FIRST 50 DJ TECHNIQUES

YOU SHOULD KNOW

by DJ Hapa

To access video, visit:
www.halleonard.com/mylibrary

Enter Code
5504-1637-1236-4927

ISBN 978-1-5400-9754-5

Visit Hal Leonard Online at
www.halleonard.com

Contact us:
Hal Leonard
7777 West Bluemound Road
Milwaukee, WI 53213
Email: info@halleonard.com

In Europe, contact:
Hal Leonard Europe Limited
42 Wigmore Street
Marylebone, London, W1U 2RN
Email: info@halleonardeurope.com

In Australia, contact:
Hal Leonard Australia Pty. Ltd.
4 Lentara Court
Cheltenham, Victoria, 3192 Australia
Email: info@halleonard.com.au

CONTENTS

ABOUT THE VIDEO To access the accompanying video tutorials for download or streaming, simply visit *www.halleonard.com/mylibrary* and enter the code from page 1 of this book.

CONCEPT 1:
BPM

WHAT is BPM?

BPM is an acronym that stands for "beats per minute." Each song has a BPM. It's a way of classifying the *tempo* of a song, or how fast or slow a song is.

For easy reference, I define a beat as a headnod. As you are listening to a track and bobbing your head to the rhythm, each headnod is a *beat*. Therefore, beats per minute indicates how many headnods there are in 60 seconds, or 1 minute.

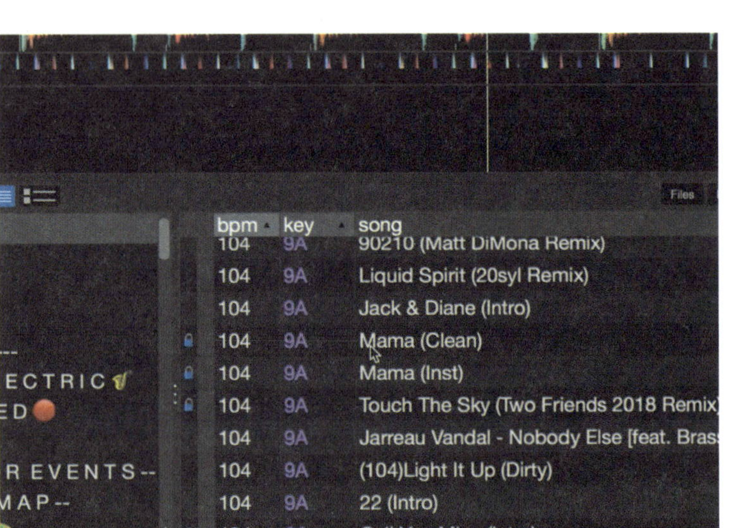

Serato DJ Pro software sorting by BPM and Key. Default sort is by Song instead of BPM.

WHY is BPM useful?

BPM determines what songs can be mixed together. I can sort by BPM in my software by clicking right next to "BPM."

We have a rule of thumb when it comes to mixing two songs together. If the BPMs of two songs are within plus or minus 4 beats of each other, then they can mix together well. If, for example, a song's BPM is 104, then I can mix it with a song that is between 100 and 108.

This is just one way I can mix between genre and era, from oldies to hip-hop, from reggae to Latin music, and so much more—all just by using BPM.

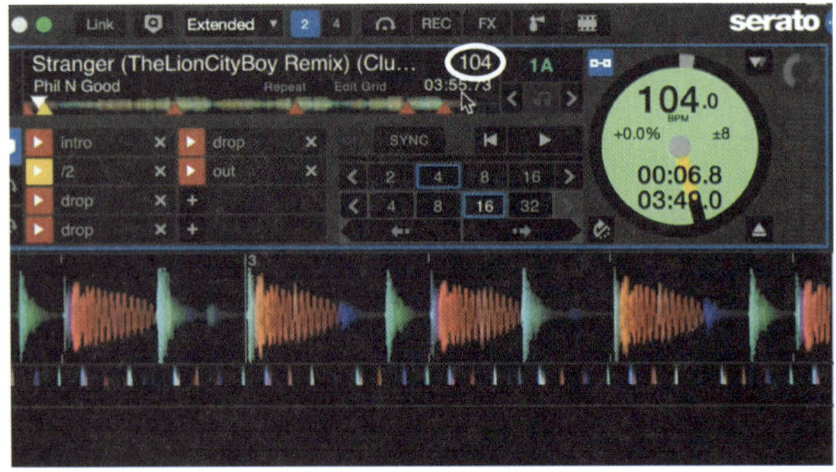

WHERE do I find BPM?

You can see the BPM number in your software. For example, in Serato, the BPM is in the large dial in the upper right-hand corner. You can also see the BPM number to the right of the track name.

What if you are not using software to find BPM? You might be using a CDJ (see Concept 46: CDJ). In that case, you can find the BPM value right on the screen.

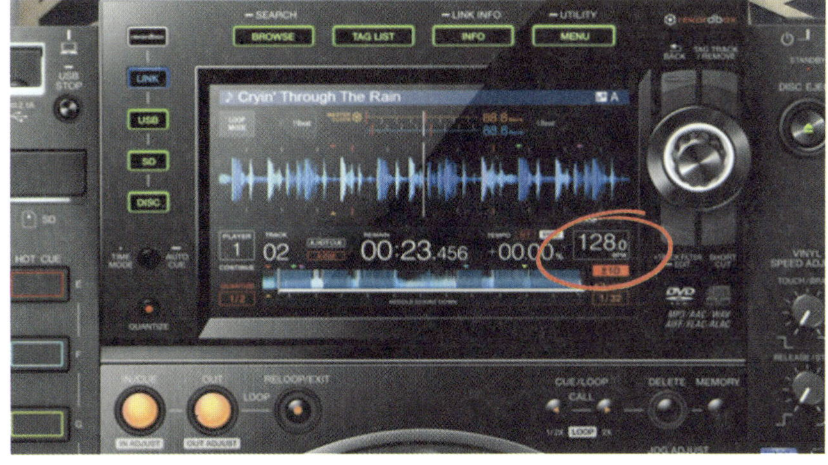

HOW do I use BPM?

Every DJ program today has an algorithm for calculating BPM. So when you download songs and put them into the software, most programs will automatically calculate the BPM. Every now and then, you'll find a song that doesn't have a BPM associated with it, or you might think that the given BPM is incorrect.

In this case, you would drag your track into the Analyze Files button. The software program will use its algorithm to figure out how far apart the drum sounds are. In the previous example, the software told us the BPM was 104. If we weren't sure about the BPM or didn't have the software to calculate it, we could download a free iPhone or Android app to help us—there are plenty to choose from. The one shown below is called Tap That Tempo.

What I am going to do is tap the phone on every headnod, or every beat. The way this app works is that it is going to average out my taps. That said, be sure to tap out the beats for as close to a minute as possible in order to have a large enough sample size to determine the BPM accurately. It is also important to move your body as you do this, to ensure accuracy and stay in the groove.

Now that you understand BPM, you can choose two songs to mix together to start building your DJ set list.

You may want to look into the following related terms in this book.

Related terms: beatmatching, tempo, grid, tempo range, basic music theory

CONCEPT 2:

Basic Music Theory

WHAT is basic music theory?

Part of music theory is how we measure musical time. In traditional time, we have seconds and minutes; in music, however, we count time with *beats*, *bars*, and *phrases*. This method is a lot more accurate and is essential when trying to describe the length of a particular part of a song.

Remember, I define a beat as a headnod. Some people define the beat by listening to the drumbeat, but that can be difficult to analyze if it's a complicated drum pattern, or when there are sections of the song where the drumbeat cuts out. It's easier to follow along with how you nod your head.

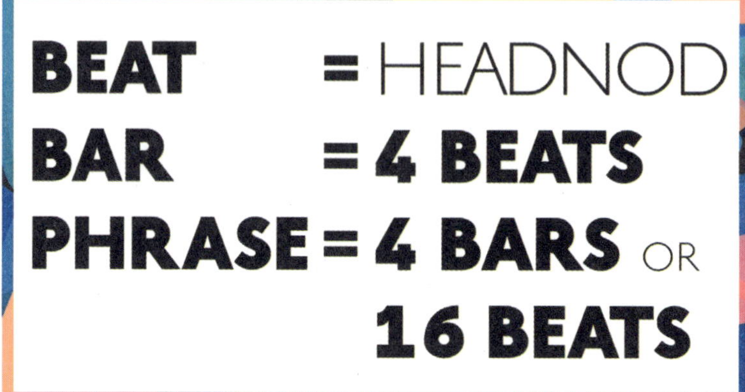

In many songs, there are 4 beats to a bar and 4 bars in a phrase. So, when we try to describe a section in a song, we need to use one of these three terms. Instead of describing the length of a chorus as 12.5 seconds, it is far more accurate to say the section is 16 beats, or 4 bars, or 1 phrase.

WHY is basic music theory useful?

DJs are primarily focused on the structure of the music as opposed to composition. We are taking songs that are already completed works and breaking them into smaller pieces that we can use creatively to make something new. DJs are looking to find points of intersection within two songs, while preserving and respecting the original structure of the music. We use the natural points between phrases to change songs and create a unique experience for the audience, seamlessly blending between songs that originally were not intended to go together.

As we focus on the structure, it is important to understand that we are not focused on the notes or how to play the notes—that is the concern of other musicians. Instead, we need to understand the structure of the tracks and how to get in and out of them (see Concept 40: Anatomy of the Mix).

WHERE do I find basic music theory?

All DJ software displays a *waveform*, which is a digital representation of the song you are playing. The software will create a grid after it analyzes the file and gives it a BPM value. Above or below the grid are usually numbers that identify the bar count. Watching the bar count on the waveform can be a great way of understanding how to count beats and bars.

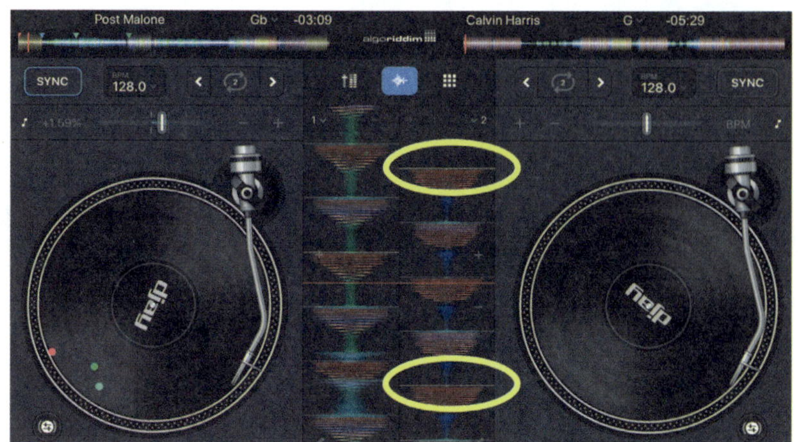

The "1" of each bar is notated with a darker yellow line on the grid.

HOW do I use basic music theory?

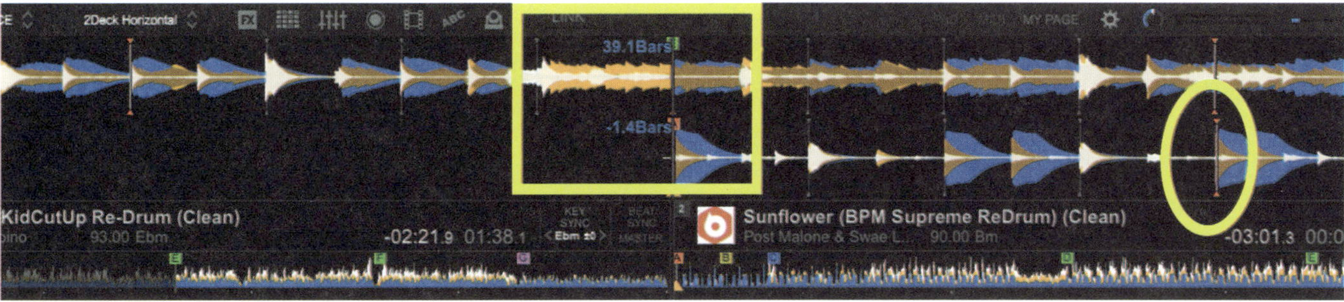

Beats and bar counter in rekordbox software

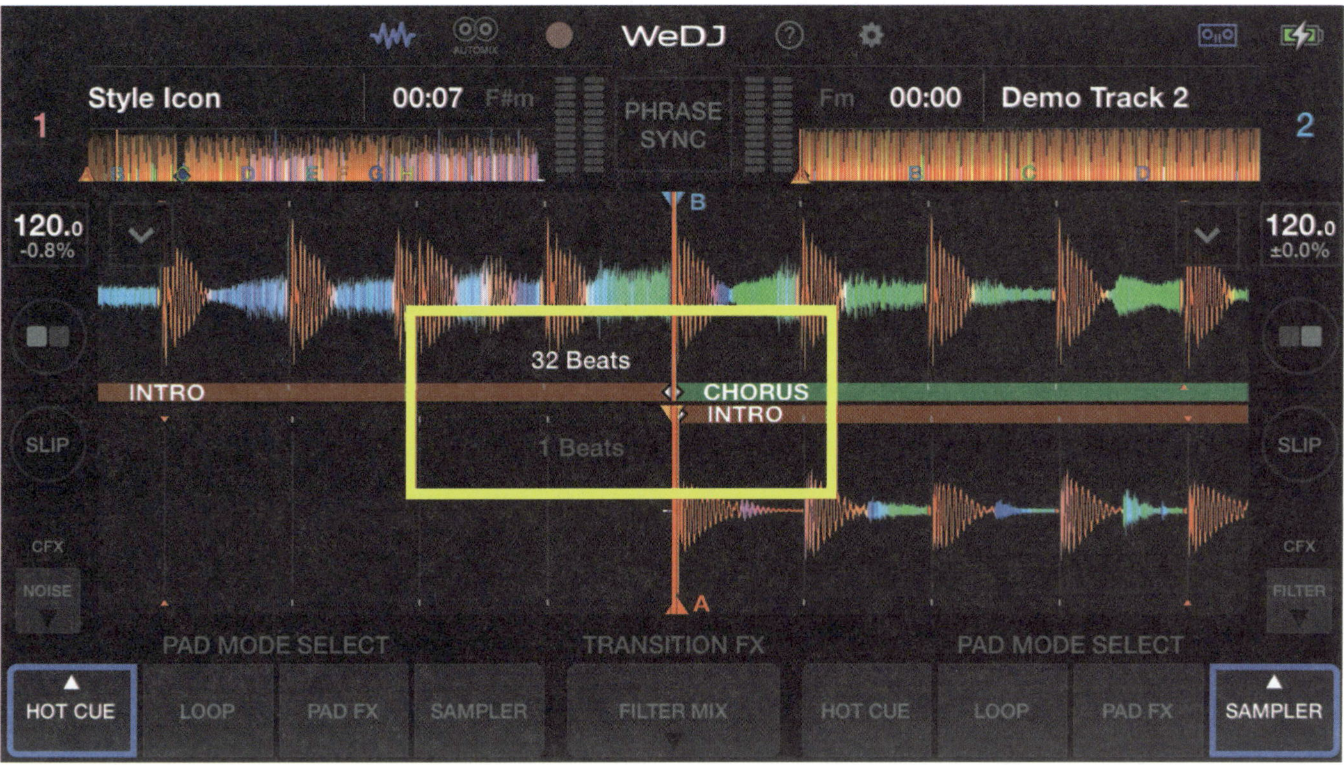

Beat countdown in WeDJ app

Being able to break down songs and understand their lengths in beats, bars, and phrases will make you a better mixing DJ. In my own career, this is what took my mixing to the next level. I was mixing professionally in nightclubs several times a week, but at times, I lacked confidence because there were songs I had no idea how to get in and out of.

I started as a drummer, and for whatever reason, I felt that the music theory I used on that instrument didn't apply when I was simply "playing" songs. I couldn't have been more wrong. Once I started to think about songs in bars and phrases, everything opened up for me. It was as if I was blind, and then *poof*—I could see.

Breaking down songs is an art that I try to teach every DJ I mentor. It starts with understanding basic music theory to the degree that you can naturally feel how long 4 bars is.

Related terms: beats, bars, phrases, measure, mixing

CONCEPT 3:

Mapping Out Songs

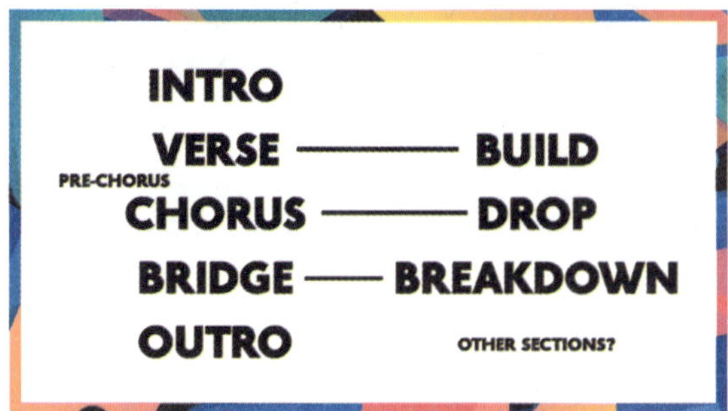

WHAT is mapping out a song?

Mapping out a song is when you break down the structure of a song, figuring out the lengths of each section in terms of beats, bars, and phrases. You are studying the song, much like a musician following sheet music, but in the case of the DJ, you are focused on the structure instead of the note composition.

Though you are able to find and do many things online, this is not one of them. This is the work you will have to do as a DJ, and figuring out the structure of the music is similar to solving a puzzle.

WHY is mapping out a song important?

You need to know the different parts of songs in order to get in and out of them during mixing. You are actually looking from the perspective of the person who produced the song. A lot of thought goes into the length of the song and its different sections, and this is part of the process of *arrangement*; you are essentially going into that headspace and unlocking it. Anyone outside the producer space will see and consume the song one way, while a DJ who studies the song sees it another way. Song structure is similar to architecture. An architect looks at a building and perceives it according to its framing and other detail elements, while the average passerby will just look at a house and see that it is tall or has three stories.

Mapping your song is knowing your music. Knowing the lengths of the parts of the song will help you figure out which pieces of Song A will fit nicely under Song B, so you can create a seamless transition between them and manage the overall energy of the dancefloor.

WHERE do I put this information?

It is key to store this information somewhere accessible while you are playing live. You will need it to jog your memory because it's nearly impossible to remember the structure of every track in your library. In the digital DJ era, you can map your songs with Hot Cues by labeling them according to length (or even changing their colors to correspond to various lengths; see Concept 19: Hot Cue Strategy). This is a great practice; however, this information will be visible only if you stick to the same DJ software. I like to write some of the important information (length of the intro, length of the first chorus) in the comment field so that information will be stored to the MP3 tag and will travel with the file to any software program. This may seem tedious, but it has saved me a ton of time and frustration, and it has allowed me to access my mapping notes even when using new DJ software.

Back in the day, we used to put stickers on the vinyl records, noting BPM or the number of bars for the intro. These notes would go directly on the record or the sleeve as a reminder. I also kept a notebook and would refer back to it; but now, in the digital DJ era, the best approach is to utilize the metadata fields in your DJ software.

Think of it like an address book or contact list in your phone. You may not remember the number of your neighbor or one of your friends, but you can go into the address book to obtain their information—whether it be their phone number, email address, or mailing address. Not to get off on a tangent, but I'm just now realizing how dependent I am on my address book in my phone!

HOW do I map out a song?

Mapping a song is something that has to be practiced. Most people haven't taken the time to break a song down structurally, but this is such a crucial part of improving your mixing.

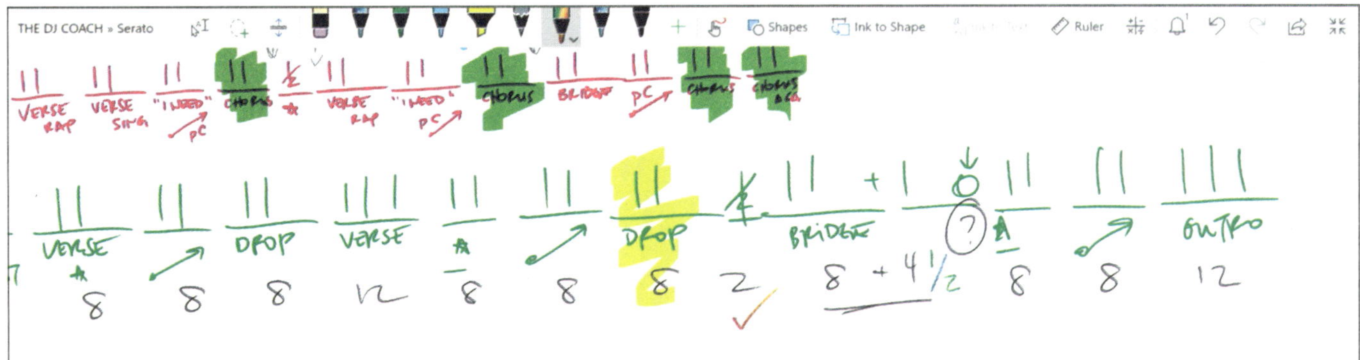

Look at the section changes. Stay focused on the structure surrounding the drums and the actual beat instead of focusing on the lyrics and melody. Also, keep in mind the bigger picture. We don't need to know the length of every section of the song. We are mostly focused on how we can get in and out of each song, so it's most important to know the lengths of the sections you'll be using to accomplish that.

If you find yourself getting lost or confused, take a step back. As a listener, you can probably feel when the song is about to go into the chorus. You can also feel when the chorus is over. Some of my students have made this process more difficult than it needs to be by obsessing over the beat and bar count. Also, keep in mind the reason we are doing this. Understanding song lengths will lead to a greater understanding of the songs you are playing, which will give you more confidence and will create more seamless transitions.

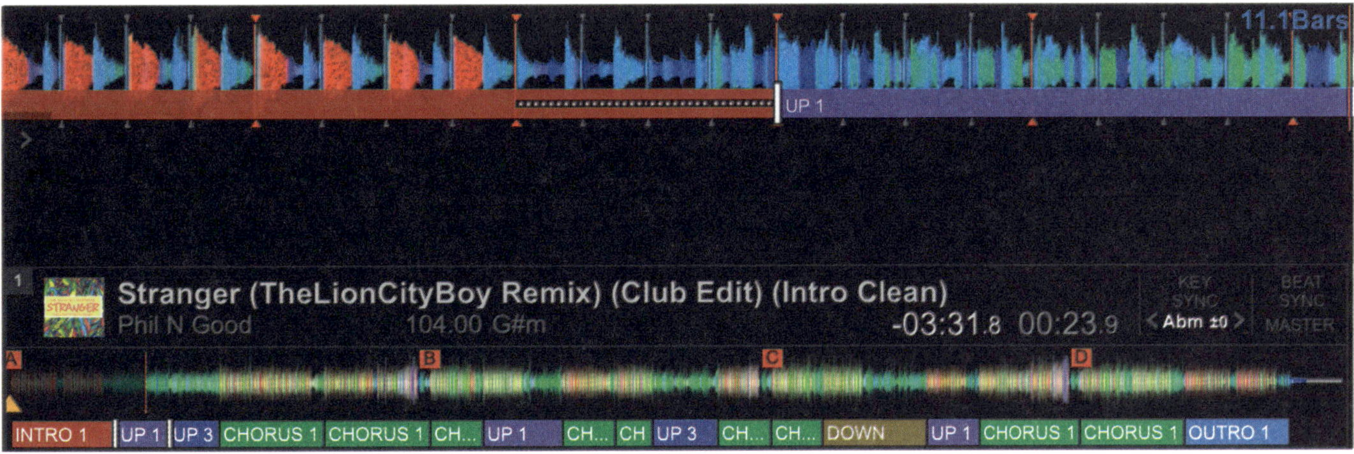

If it doesn't come easy at first, don't worry. This is not something I did when I first started out, but since I have applied this, my mixing has improved exponentially!

Related terms: hot cues, grid, song structure, mixing, Anatomy of the Mix

CONCEPT 4:
EQ

WHAT is EQ?

Equalization (commonly referred to as *EQ*) is defined as the process of changing the balance of different frequency components in an audio signal. When utilizing your DJ equipment, there are different knobs that control or isolate the different frequencies. Most DJ equipment features a three-band EQ, controlling the high, medium (mid), and low frequencies. Think of these knobs as "volume" for the different frequencies.

This is comparable to the equalizer on a car stereo. Usually there are presets for jazz, pop, or dance, etc. These presets use treble (high frequency), mid, and bass (low frequency) to increase or decrease the frequencies for the best settings based on genre.

Human ears can detect a wide range of frequencies, anywhere from 20 Hz to 20 kHz.

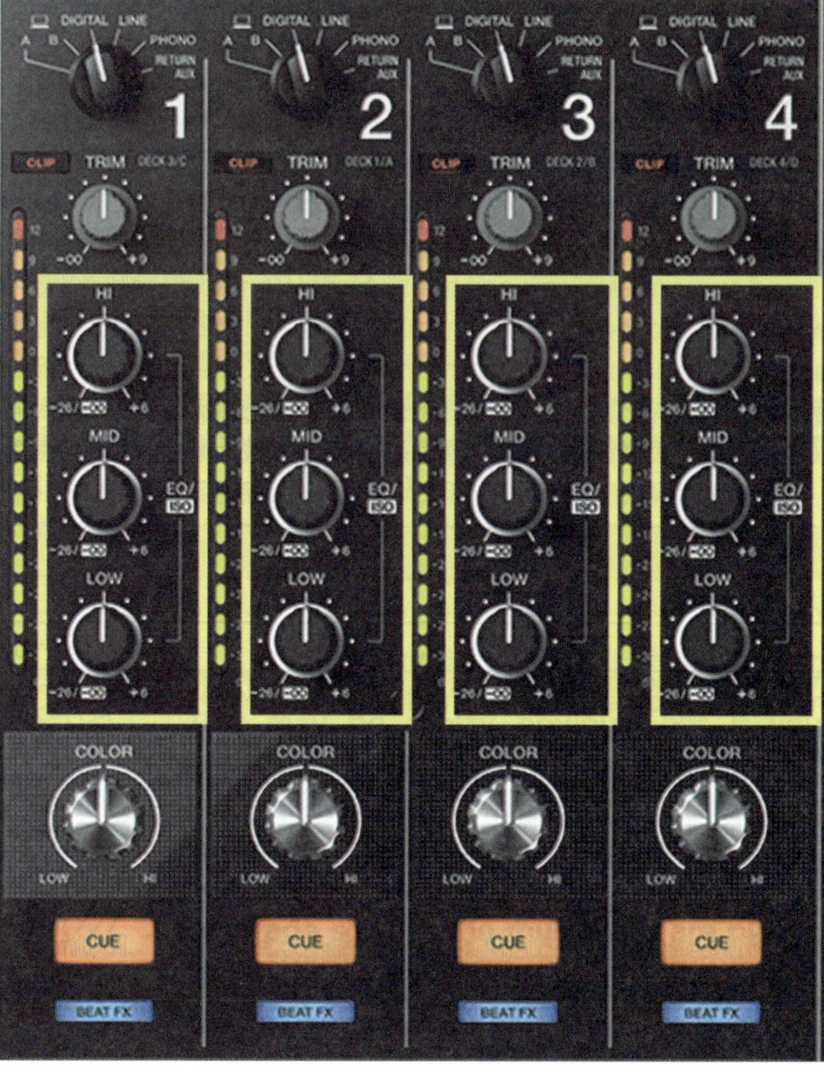

EQ knobs on a Pioneer DJM-900NXS2 mixer

WHY is EQ useful?

EQ is used to change the dynamics in a song. When mixing or layering two songs on top of one another, you have double the frequencies, and this will cause the mix to be louder and possibly distorted. In order to smooth out the mix, we can utilize our EQ (along with our channel volume) to help minimize the stacking of frequencies.

WHERE do I find EQ?

A mixer will have EQ controls for each of the input channels. These are either a set of knobs or a set of faders. In the adjacent image, you can see the fader controls organized vertically on the controller, where the high level of each frequency is toward the top of each fader, and

EQ faders in Algoriddim djay Pro software

the low level of each frequency is toward the bottom. Many frequency controls are displayed similarly to this; however, the displays on other mixers or DJ software programs may vary slightly.

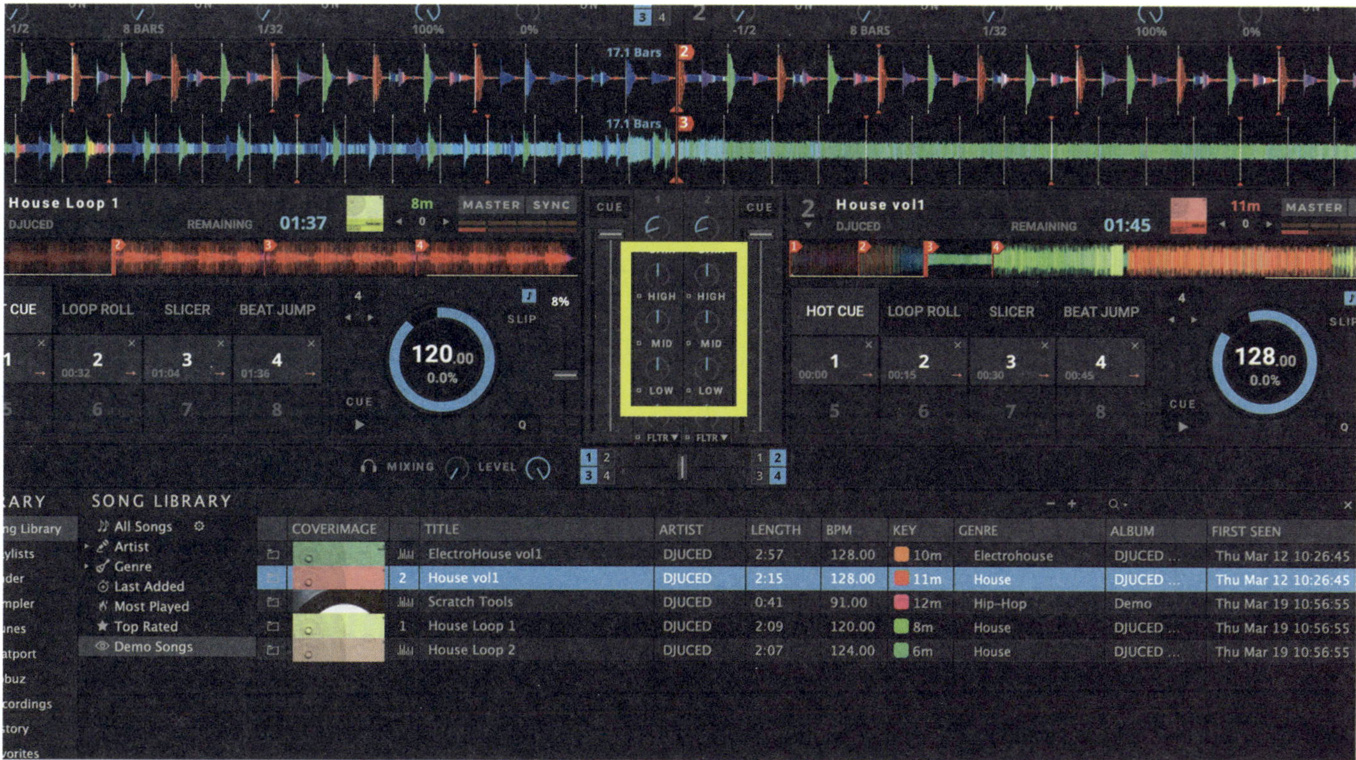

EQ knobs in DJUCED software

HOW do I use EQ?

There is typically a notch in the fader or knob, which is the original position of the frequency. If you move the controller down or to the left, you are taking the frequency away. If you move it up or to the right, you are adding to the frequency. I highly recommend that you do not turn these all the way up or to the right, as this will over-amplify the frequency and create unwanted distortion in your sound.

When mixing songs together, as you turn one frequency up in Song A, it's helpful to turn down that same frequency in Song B. A lot of this is also based on feel and varies depending on the two songs you are mixing together. For example, say you are mixing an acapella song over an instrumental song. Most likely, there are not a lot of low-end frequencies in the acapella song, so you won't have to worry about those conflicting with the low end of the instrumental. However, when mixing two beats or full songs together, you'll always want to adjust the EQ of each so that the two songs blend together as smoothly as possible.

We have a step-by-step breakdown of this in Concept 32: Smoothing Out the Mix.

Related terms: high frequency, mid frequency, low frequency, preventing distortion

CONCEPT 5:
Inputs

WHAT are inputs?

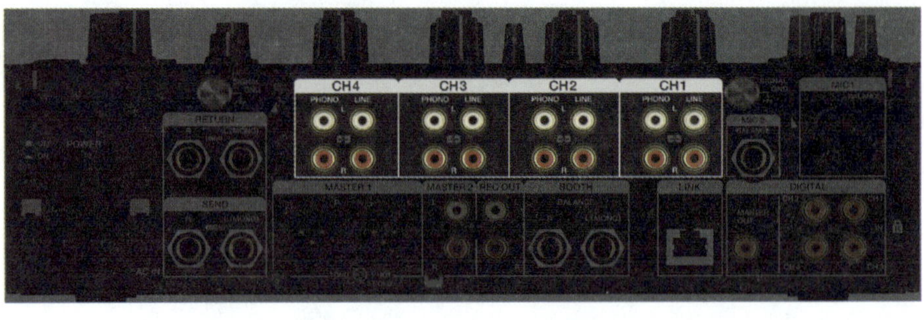

All audio and visual equipment has inputs and outputs. Understanding this basic signal flow is crucial for DJing, especially during setup or when sound is not coming out of your equipment properly. A typical DJ setup will have turntables or CDJs that need to be plugged into the mixer. On the back of the mixer is a set of inputs and outputs. Most of the inputs on a DJ mixer are for RCA connections.

NAME	USE OF INPUT	XLR	1/4	RCA	1/8
PHONO	Phonograph input for vinyl turntables			X	
CD/LINE	Line Level input for CDJ or any other digital audio equipment			X	
DIGITAL	Coaxial input for hi-fi digital audio equipment			X	
AUX IN	Additional input for digital audio equipment			X	
MIC	Microphone	X	X		

WHY are inputs useful?

Inputs are useful when you have multiple devices connected. Depending on your setup, you may not need to worry about inputs. For example, if you are plugging in your laptop to a simple DJ controller, you likely don't need to plug in any inputs; there may not even *be* any inputs on the back of your controller. However, a larger audio mixing board might have up to 40 inputs (though it would be difficult to DJ on a mixing board like this).

A 2-channel mixer is our standard, or most basic, DJ mixer. This will allow us to mix two audio sources at the same time. Originally, the basic DJ rig consisted of two vinyl turntables plugged into a 2-channel DJ mixer. The mixer allowed the DJ to control the volume independently of each input. Before DJ equipment was created, DJs used two different audio receivers and plugged each turntable into the different receivers. Each receiver had a volume knob for controlling the audio. Now, we have specific equipment designed for this same use. By having multiple inputs, we are able to play songs simultaneously and blend and mix them together!

A 4-channel mixer will allow us to have four inputs and play four pieces of audio simultaneously. The 2- and 4-channel mixers are the most common in the DJ world.

2-channel mixer inputs

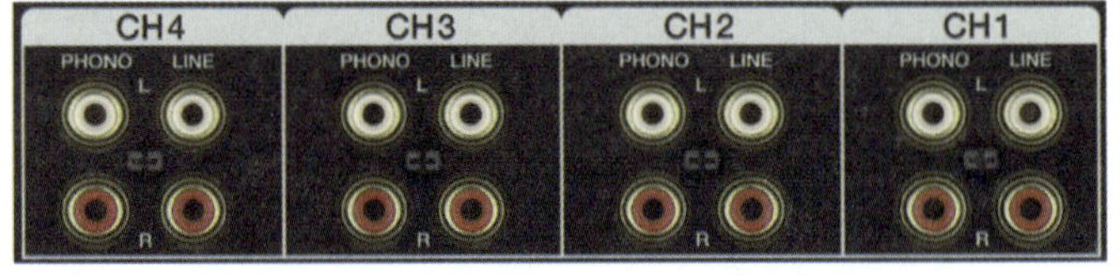

4-channel mixer inputs

WHERE do I find inputs?

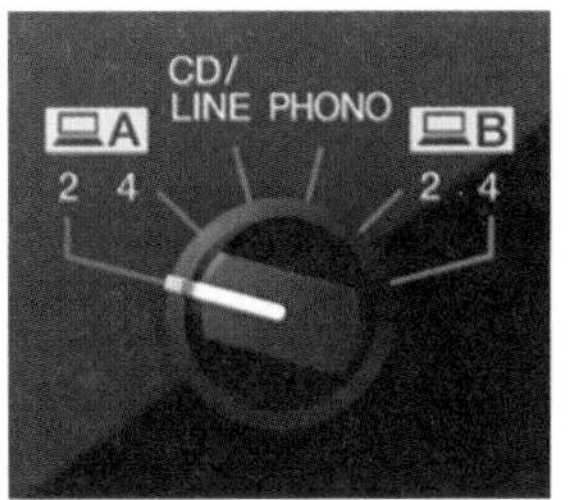

You will find the inputs on the back of the hardware and the input will display a number that corresponds to the input selector. The different inputs are used for different types of audio devices. For instance, a Phono input is reserved for a "phonograph" player, or vinyl turntable. CD/Line is reserved for a CD player, multimedia player, or any line-level device, which is essentially anything except a vinyl turntable or microphone.

In this digital DJ era, your mixer can even have an input for a USB cable, so you can connect it to your laptop. Mixers have become more robust and are equipped with digital audio sound cards that make them compatible with the DJ software on your laptop. When playing from Serato DJ Pro, for example, the input switch above should be switched to the position that is pictured. I have my laptop plugged into USB A and I am trying to control Deck 2 with Channel 2.

HOW do I use inputs?

Input switches are commonly found at the top of the mixer. This works similarly to how your television works. On your TV, you have a button to toggle between HDMI 1, HDMI 2, etc., to ensure that the signal is coming through. If you aren't seeing your AppleTV or XBOX properly, it's likely because you need to change the input selector. It works the same way with a DJ mixer. There are typically two types of RCA inputs for a channel on a DJ mixer: Phono or Line.

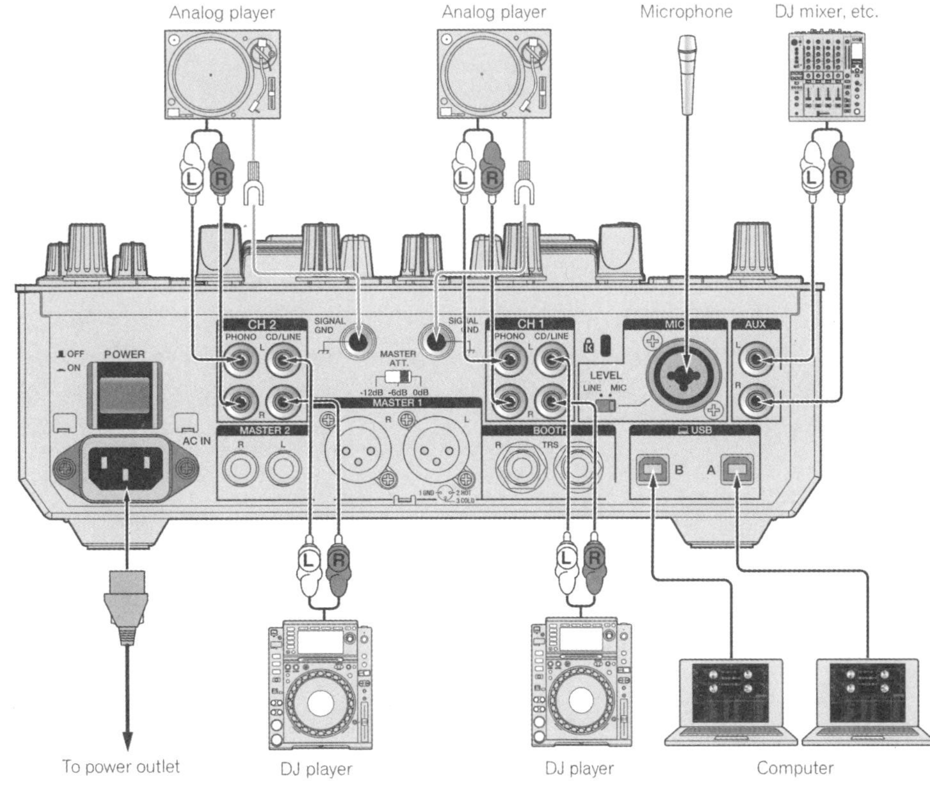

As mentioned above, a Phono input is reserved for plugging in a vinyl turntable. This input amplifies the phono signal, which can be as much as 1000 times lower in volume than a Line signal! At times, the DJ mixer can also be referred to as a "pre-amp" since it amplifies the phono signal. If you accidently plug your phone or any other digital signal that is already amplified into a phono input, what would happen? It would be amplifying something that does not need to be amplified and will severely distort the sound!

As mentioned earlier, we need to ensure that the input switcher on the mixer is set to the same input number that we plugged our device into. As with the TV, if we are on the wrong input, we won't hear anything.

Related terms: Phono, Line, AUX, outputs, mic controls

CONCEPT 6:
Mic Controls

WHAT are mic controls?

A *mic*, or microphone, is an instrument for converting sound waves into electrical energy variations that may then be amplified, transmitted, or recorded. As a DJ, it is another input and is considered a dedicated input. Most DJ controllers have a microphone input with a variety of controls, such as volume and EQ. Many of you may remember the reference of "two turntables and a microphone" as the definition of what a DJ needs (popularized by the Beck song "Where It's At").

Volume for the microphone, sometimes referred to as Gain, is usually located on the top of the mixer and is usually near the mic input.

Some mixers have a Talk Over button that will automatically duck the music, making what you are saying on the mic louder than what is playing.

There may also be a separate set of EQ controls for the microphone; although, with most DJ mixers, High and Low is common, but a Mid control for the microphone is not.

WHY are mic controls useful?

The DJ was originally the "master of the ceremony" (MC), who is controlling the music, making announcements in between songs, or simply keeping the energy level up and inserting one's voice and personality. I like to break using a microphone into two distinct parts:

Part 1: Technical

The technical part of using a microphone is incredibly important to understand and master, regardless of whether or not you are in favor of using a mic in your own performance. There will be times when you will be required to jump on a microphone or be able to activate a microphone for someone else. (See Concept 7: Preventing Mic Feedback.)

Part 2: Creative

The microphone can be a very useful tool in your performance. It signifies control and confidence and also creates a human connection with the crowd. There is an art to using a microphone and finding your own voice. Glossophobia, or the fear of public speaking, affects millions of people! Some ways to get over this are knowing your material, practicing, and using visualization techniques.

Certain DJs, like Kid Capri from New York, are known to use the mic effectively. His use of the mic is a big part of his performance.

WHERE do I find mic controls?

The mic controls are usually close to the top-left or top-right corner of your controller—out of the way of the mixing controls. Occasionally, the mic controls are located on the front or back of DJ mixers and controllers.

HOW do I use mic controls?

Using the microphone appropriately and effectively is an important part of DJing. It is best to talk over an instrumental section and not over vocals. You can also utilize the volume controls to lower the music, or use the Talk Over control so your voice becomes the prominent audio.

Make sure your mic volume is slightly louder than the music so your voice can cut through. This is different from mixing your voice into the audio as you would if you were a singer. It's also important to use the mic EQ to fit your voice. For example, if you know you are lacking a little bass in your voice, you can turn the bass EQ up a bit.

It's also really important that you don't turn the mic gain up too high, as it will increase the field of sound that the mic is picking up and can create a *feedback loop* (high-pitched sound). If you find that the mic volume is too low, be sure to check the overall master volume on your mixer; turning that up will turn up *all* your inputs—including the mic—without widening the mic input field and risking feedback.

Related terms: mic feedback, gain, Talk Over, EQ, anti-feedback

CONCEPT 7:

Preventing Mic Feedback

WHAT is mic feedback?

Microphone feedback is a positive gain loop between a microphone and a loudspeaker. Speakers amplify the mic signal, and then the microphone picks up the sound from the speakers. This creates a high-pitched sound that is not pleasant to hear *at all*. This is also a tell-tale sign that the DJ is not in control of the event, so it's best to avoid feedback at all costs and to understand how it happens.

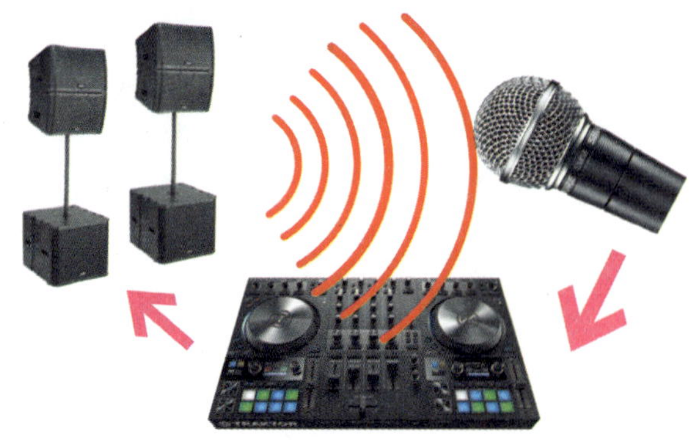

WHY is preventing mic feedback useful?

Mic feedback is one of the most annoying sounds you can hear and is a strong indication that something is wrong. You need to be able to fix the problem when mic feedback occurs, or better yet, prevent it from happening in the first place. If you create feedback and are not able to fix it fast, an audience will look negatively on your DJ skills—no matter how good you are at mixing and song selection!

WHEN do I get mic feedback?

Mic feedback is usually generated from common mistakes. If you are standing too close to the speaker and the sensitivity range of the mic is too wide, feedback can happen. The way to prevent this is to understand what type of microphone you are using and what its polar field is.

Some mics have the option to select or change the polar field. However, most simple microphones for live performance are cardioid mics. This is important to understand so that you know how and where the microphone is picking up sound. If the field is larger, there is a higher possibility for feedback.

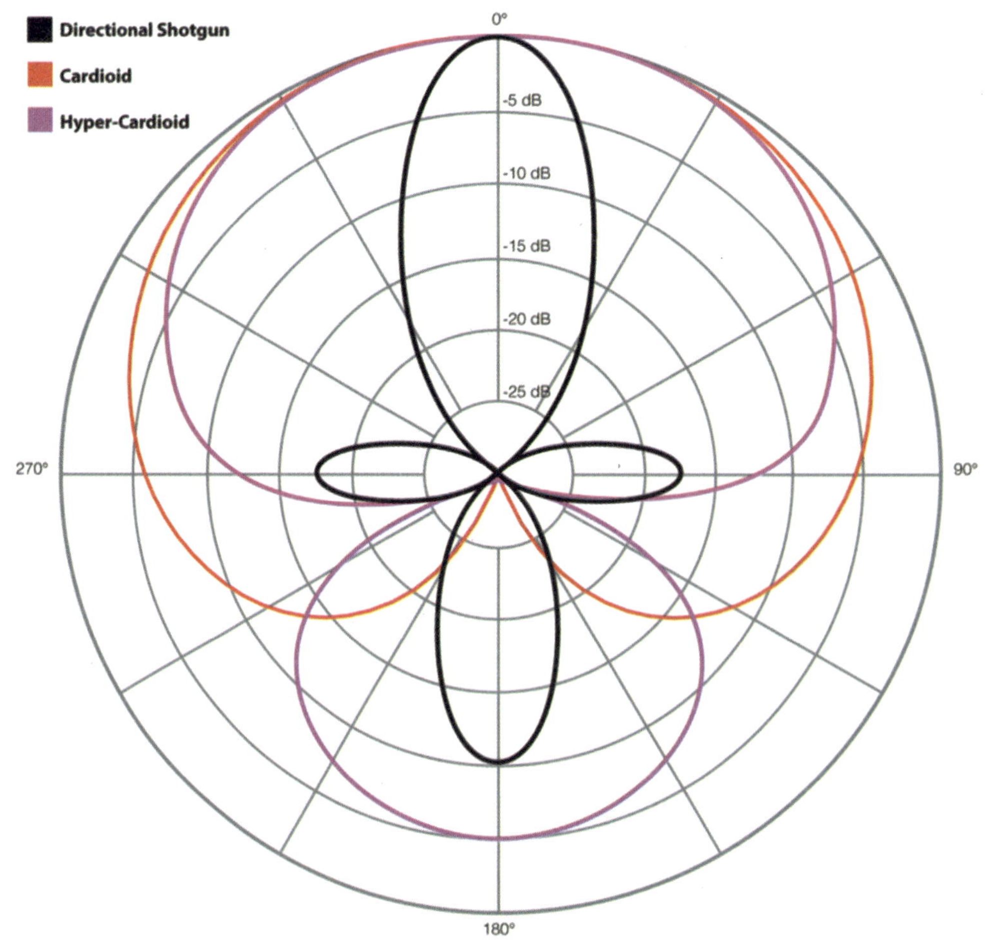

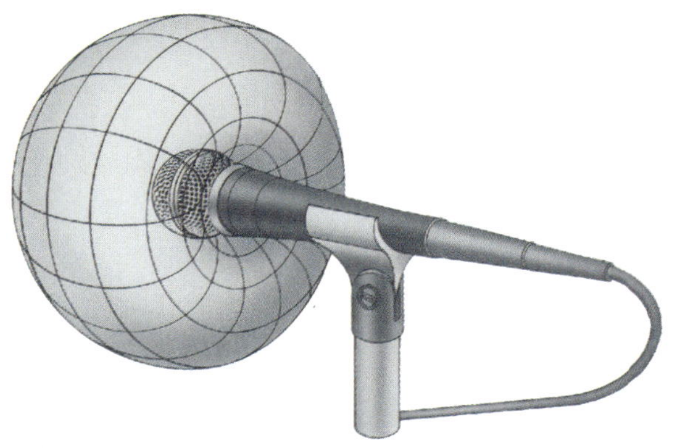

The location of the mic in relation to your mouth is a key factor as well. A big mistake made by DJs and people making speeches is holding the mic too far from their mouths. This is a pretty common scenario, especially at weddings and private events where people who aren't typically used to handling a microphone are asked to deliver a speech. In these scenarios, when the DJ realizes the audience is having trouble hearing, they may turn up the gain, which increases the field. So, now you're able to hear the speech better, but it's because you increased the field. Any sound that travels into that field will now get picked up as well, creating a higher possibility for unwanted feedback.

Cupping the mic will also create feedback because you are not allowing the air to travel outward, which will create an echo chamber and, hence, feedback.

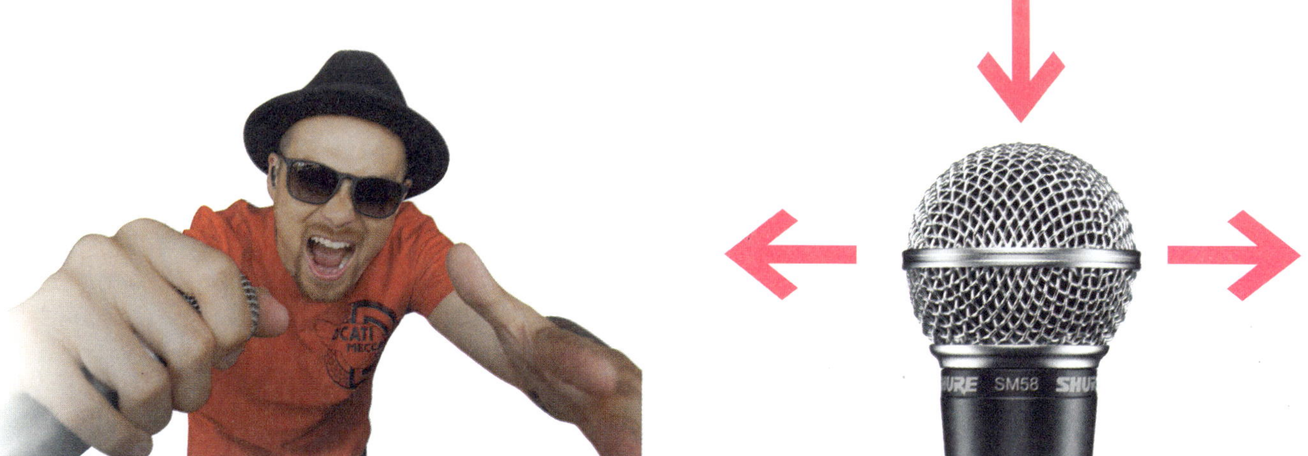

HOW do I prevent mic feedback?

Just as we spoke about what creates mic feedback, eliminating those actions will help eliminate the possibility of feedback.

- **Don't stand too close to the speaker.** Allow some air between the speaker and the mic.
- **Make sure you understand how to use the mic.** Train others how to use it as well.
- **Do not cup the mic.** Allow a little distance between the mic and your mouth, again allowing for the sound to travel instead of creating that echo chamber mentioned above.

Follow the guidelines above and the mic will be a great tool for keeping your crowd engaged and entertained.

Related terms: mic controls, gain, anti-feedback, speaker placement, different types of mic fields

CONCEPT 8:

Outputs

WHAT are outputs?

Outputs are the opposite of inputs. In order to get sound to the speaker, you will need to understand the outputs from your DJ rig. DJ mixers and controllers typically have several outputs: Master, Booth, AUX, and Headphones. The master output goes to the speakers. The booth output is reserved for a monitor that would be with you in the "DJ Booth." The AUX output is an optional output sometimes used for recording or sending to another device. In some cases, this can also be referred to as a "Zone Out." Headphone output is for the pre-cue in your headphones. Understanding the different outputs on your mixer or controller is important because you have to know which cable connections you need. Typically, the more professional the gear, the more options there are for outputs. For example, most controllers under $300 have only RCA outputs, which are typically found on home audio equipment; whereas mixers and controllers over $1000 typically have more professional audio outputs with XLR connections.

NAME	USE OF OUTPUT	XLR	1/4	RCA	1/8
MASTER	Main speakers	X	X	X	
BOOTH	Monitor speaker for DJ		X		
AUX OUT	Auxiliary output for recording device or to send to another mixer			X	
REC OUT	Record output dedicated for recording device			X	
HEADPHONES	Pre-Cue for headphones		X		X

WHY are outputs useful?

Each output has a separate volume control. This is extremely helpful if you have different zones and want to have different volumes in these separate places. For example, you may want to keep the booth monitor quieter, with the master volume loud for the crowd.

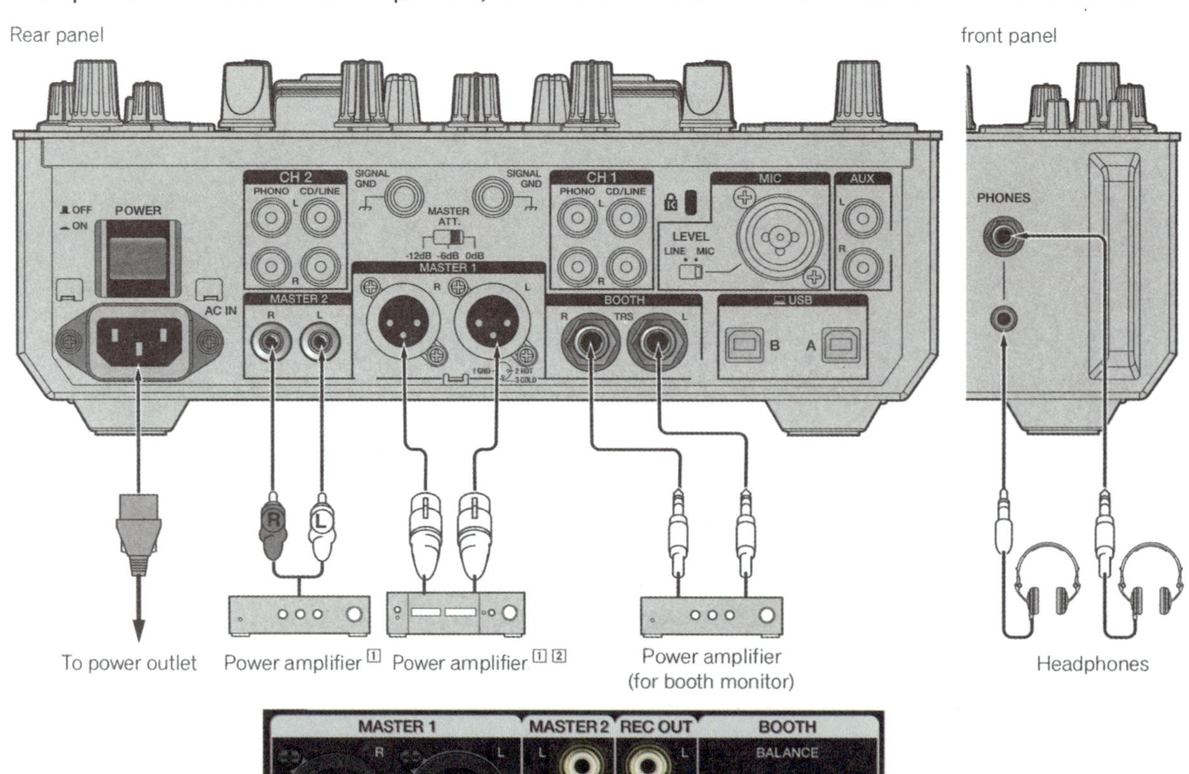

WHERE are the outputs?

The master and booth outputs are usually at the back of the mixer. Headphone outputs are located on top or at the front of the mixer. Everything is labeled much like the inputs.

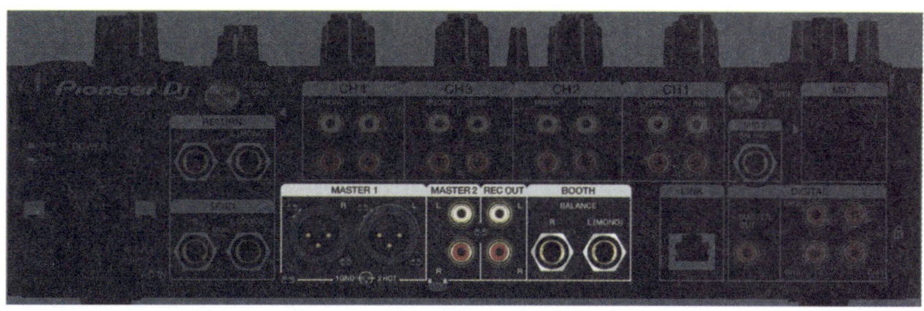

HOW do I use outputs?

When setting up, one of the most important things to remember is to keep your volume knobs down when plugging in cables for your outputs. If the volume is up, you have the potential of blowing out a speaker or, at the very least, creating an alarming noise. After you have plugged in, and you are sending a signal through the mixer, you should be able to see on the LEDs that sound is coming through. Then, you can steadily raise the volume to the desired level. Keep in mind that an empty room sounds much different from one filled with people, so it's important to keep checking in throughout the night to be sure that your sound is loud enough.

Learning the different cable connections is very important as you need to make sure you have the correct cables for your equipment. Without the proper cables, you won't be able to connect to speakers and rock the party!

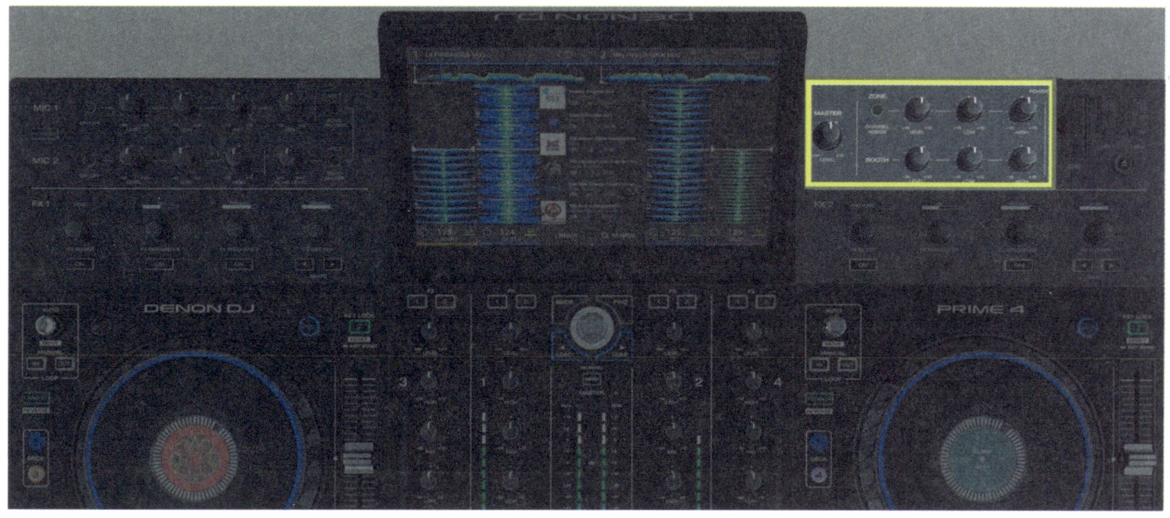

Denon DJ Prime 4 with a unique XLR Zone Out in addition to Booth and Master outs

Related terms: cables, XLR, 1/4", RCA, Record Out, TRS, speakers

CONCEPT 9:

Cables

WHAT are cables?

Cables are insulated wires used for transmitting electricity and, in the case of a DJ, sound and music. There are four different types of audio cables that are most common: XLR, RCA, 1/4", and 1/8". They are used for inputs and outputs, and you need to know the right terminology in order to connect them.

Cables are designed with two different connectors: *male* and *female*. The female connector is generally a receptacle that receives and holds the male connector.

For example:

- An XLR female to a 1/4" male is a typical wired microphone cable.
- A pair of RCA males and male 1/4" can go from your mixer via the Booth Out.
- An RCA male to RCA male can connect your CDJ to your mixer input.

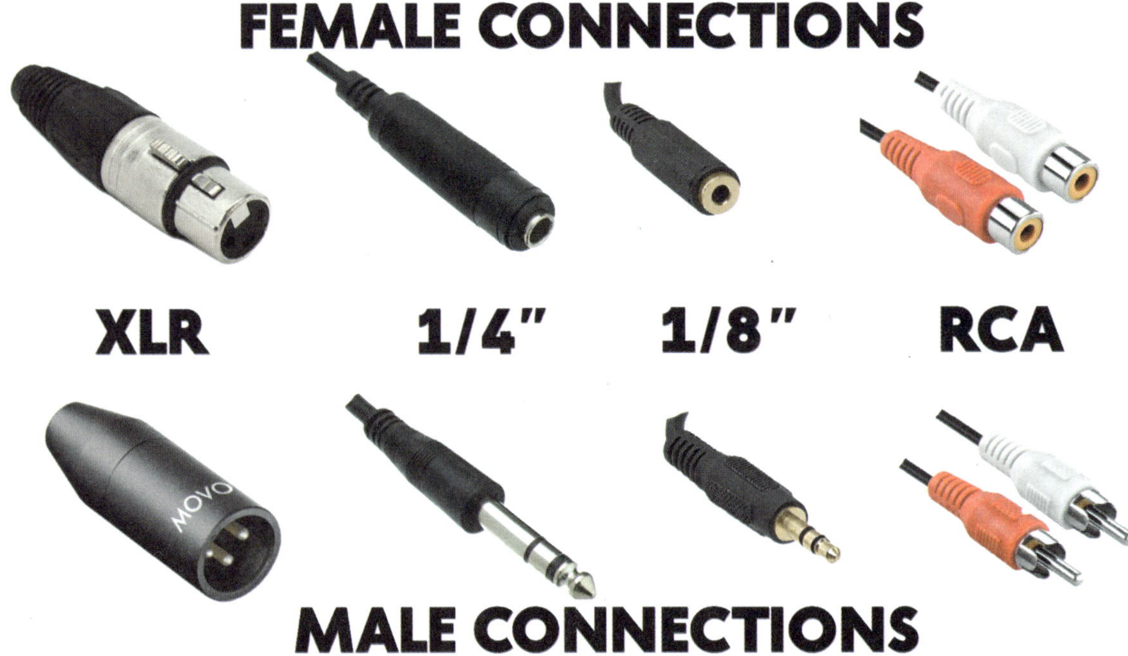

In the digital DJ era, we are also dealing with computers that work with our audio equipment. Some laptops and desktops take a USB A connection, while newer laptops require a USB C connection. There are different connectors and hubs you can use to convert these, but it's helpful to understand what these connections are called.

WHY are different types of cables useful?

Having different types of cables is useful because it allows for multiple connections. When showing up at a venue, it is necessary to have backup cables and connectors.

Also, cables can deteriorate over time. When the wires in a cable get bent—which can happen easily when gear is packed up improperly—you can break the inner wiring. Over time, most cables have the risk of deteriorating, but learning how to wrap cables properly will help prolong their life.

WHEN do I need a new cable?

Sometimes, you can actually see the loss of optimal structure in the cables and the fray of wires. In terms of sound, you may only hear one side of the audio, or sometimes you will hear a crackling sound. If you are hearing only one side, then that's your cue that half of the cable is not working properly. For example, the red part, or right side of your RCA cable is bad when you hear a low hum, buzz, or no music coming out of the right side.

HOW do I preserve my cables?

Wrapping your cables properly before and after a function or gig, as well as arranging them and securing their placement with care on-site, is the key to preserving your cables. The old school method of wrapping the extension cord around your elbow is really not the way to wrap your cables. It is best to wrap them in a circular fashion with some room in the size of the circle, so as to maintain the shape and length of the cable as much as possible. It is important to make sure that the cable is not getting twisted up; you can feel the tautness of a cord when it starts to twist. Use Velcro ties for each cable to keep the natural shape and ensure there are no kinks and there is no stress on the wiring.

Some companies offer lifetime guarantees for their cables. You may try to save money by purchasing cables without the guarantee, but the lifetime guarantee could save you money in the long run. With cables, it's not a matter of "if" they will break down, but "when."

Related terms: cables, XLR, 1/4", RCA, Record Out, TRS, speakers

CONCEPT 10:

Distortion

WHAT is distortion?

Technically, distortion is any deviation in the shape of an audio waveform between two points in a signal path. In the world of DJing, this is when there is too much sound. This happens when the input is too high and you are pushing the sound too hard into the mixer or speaker.

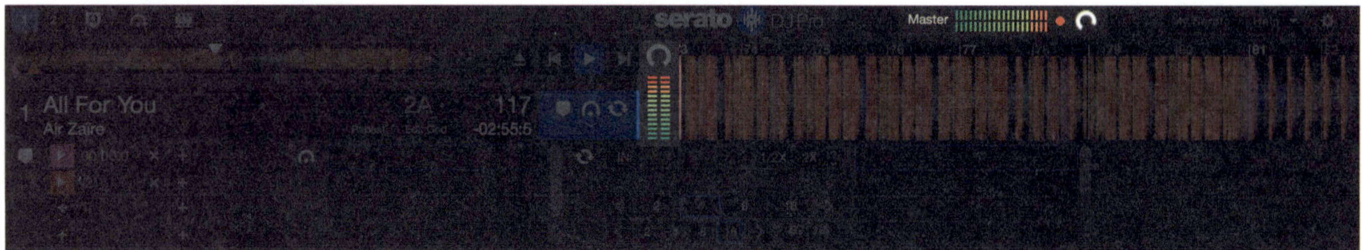

WHY is preventing distortion useful?

Just as you want to avoid mic feedback, distortion is an equally horrible sound. No matter how great your mixing is or how popular the song is that you are playing for your audience, if the sound is distorted, it will not sound good and will not have the same positive effect.

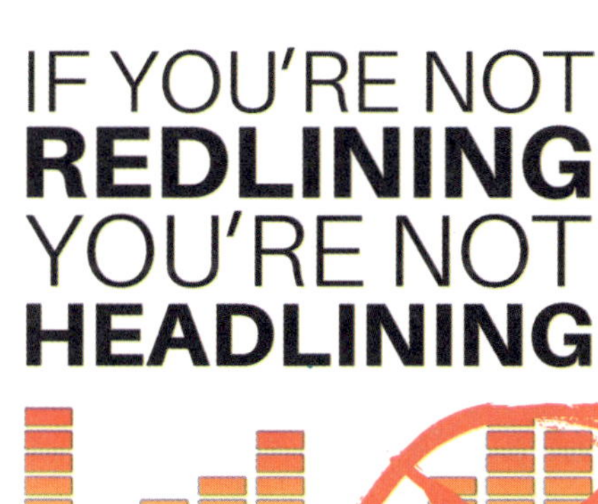

There is a saying that floats around the DJ community: "If you're not redlining, you're not headlining." This is referring to the LED meters on the mixer. When the LED is in the "red," the sound has a high probability of distorting. The "headlining" act at a festival or nightclub is usually the anticipated DJ and likely the DJ with more skills and a bigger name. This saying, while catchy, is completely false. Skilled DJs, in addition to being able to creatively mix and perform, also know how to manage their volume levels to avoid distortion.

WHERE does distortion come from?

Distortion was originally the sound of a guitar with the edges of its sound waves compressed. Guitarists would turn up the volume on their amps to the point where there was too much electricity flowing through its circuits and the original wave would come out differently.

Volume should be increased outside-in. If you have 50 people in a room who need to escape through one door, they will break down the door because everyone will be rushing through one small opening. You can look at sound in the same way—you actually need to "widen the opening" for the sound to come out properly.

On the audio side, first turn up the amplifier to the speaker's level, then turn up the master volume on your mixer; and if you need more sound, then you can start to turn up your gain.

DJs often make the mistake of turning up what's closest to them first, in other words, the gain and mixer levels. This is one of the most common ways that DJs create distortion.

The LED display measures how much sound is coming out in different levels with the colors green, yellow, and red. As mentioned, *redlining* refers to when you are pushing too much sound out. It is better to play music at a lower volume that is clear than to have it much louder but obviously distorted.

Sometimes, the issue is not with any of your settings on the mixer, but rather with the file you are using. This is certainly possible with versions of MP3s floating around the Internet that have been distorted by a DJ or producer that edited it. Make sure to remove these types of files from your library and replace them with higher quality files.

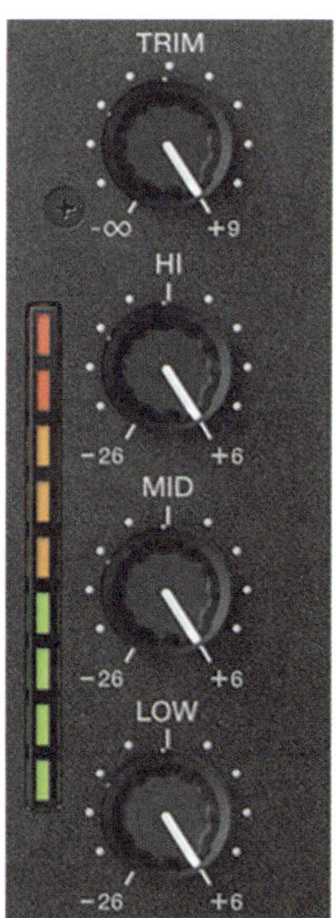

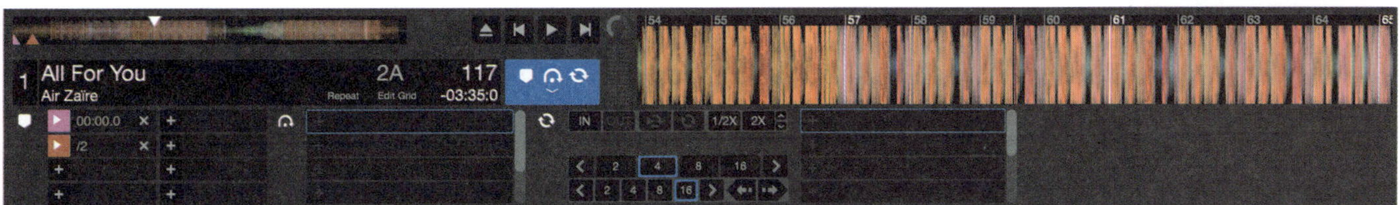

HOW do I prevent distortion?

Here's how you can prevent distortion:

1. Check your LED meters to ensure you aren't redlining in your software.
2. Make sure your individual channels aren't redlining.
3. Make sure your master output isn't redlining.
4. Finally, make sure that your amp going to your speakers isn't redlining.

If you think the volume is too low and need to turn it up, follow these steps:

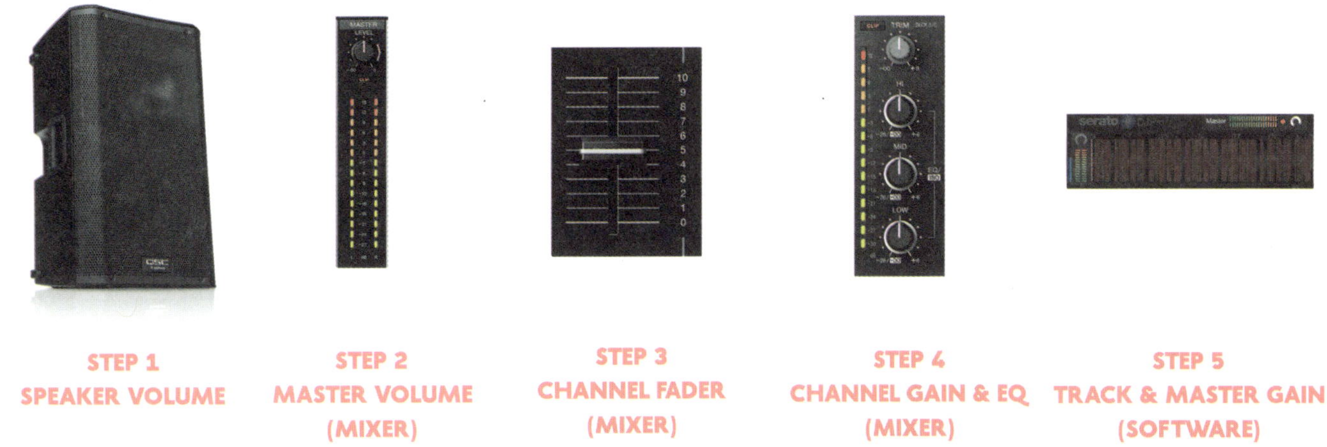

Related terms: speakers, EQ, master volume, mic controls

CONCEPT 11:

Choosing Speakers

WHAT are different types of speakers?

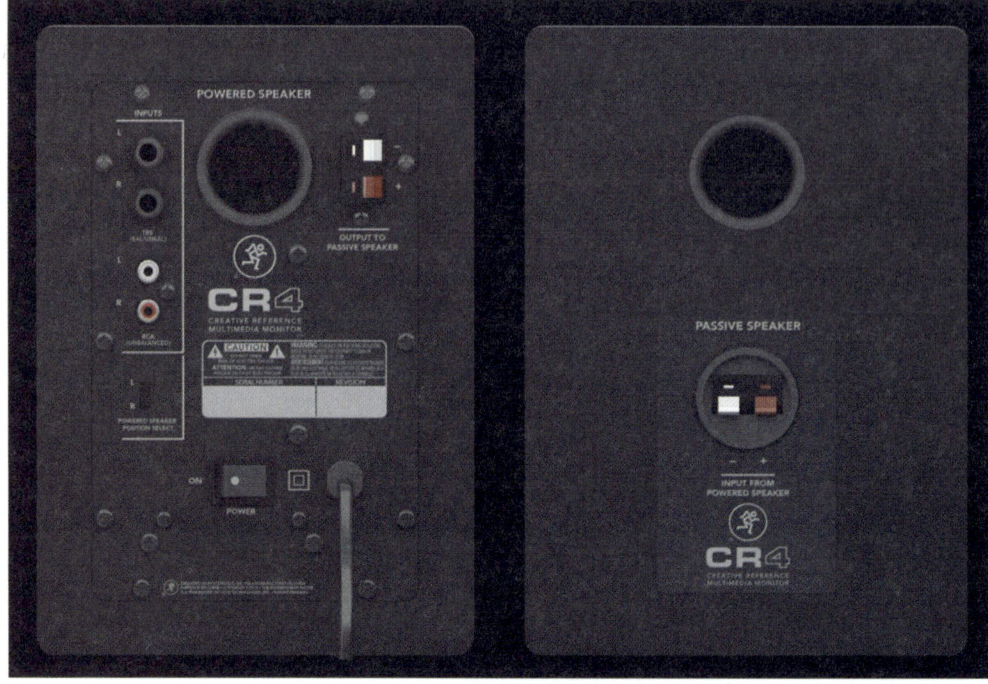

There are two kinds of speakers, *active* (or *powered*) and *passive*. Passive speakers do not have an amplifier, so you would need to buy one separately.

A DJ who is going to have a mobile system should have active speakers, as they are much easier to set up.

Bluetooth speakers can be used, however, there tends to be a latency in sending out the sound. Although Bluetooth can be convenient, at the time of writing this book, there is significant latency, especially when trying to mix music live. In addition, most professional DJ mixers and controllers do not have Bluetooth outputs. Professional level speakers are starting to have Bluetooth capability but really should be used only to play something from your mobile device.

A *subwoofer* is designed specifically for low-end frequencies. If you want a more powerful or dynamic sound, investing in a subwoofer is recommended. Some types of music, like hip-hop or EDM, have a strong low end, and the experience is completely enhanced with a dedicated subwoofer.

Tops are usually 2-way speakers that have a woofer and a *tweeter*, which is designed for the high-end frequencies. There are also 3-way speakers that have a woofer, mid, and tweeter—but having a dedicated subwoofer will give you the low-end frequencies that would be missing in these tops.

WHY are different types of speakers useful?

Some events (like cocktail receptions) don't require a subwoofer. Bluetooth is a good solution for some situations in which you need more portability. Understanding speakers as described earlier will help determine how each can be useful, given your event or situation.

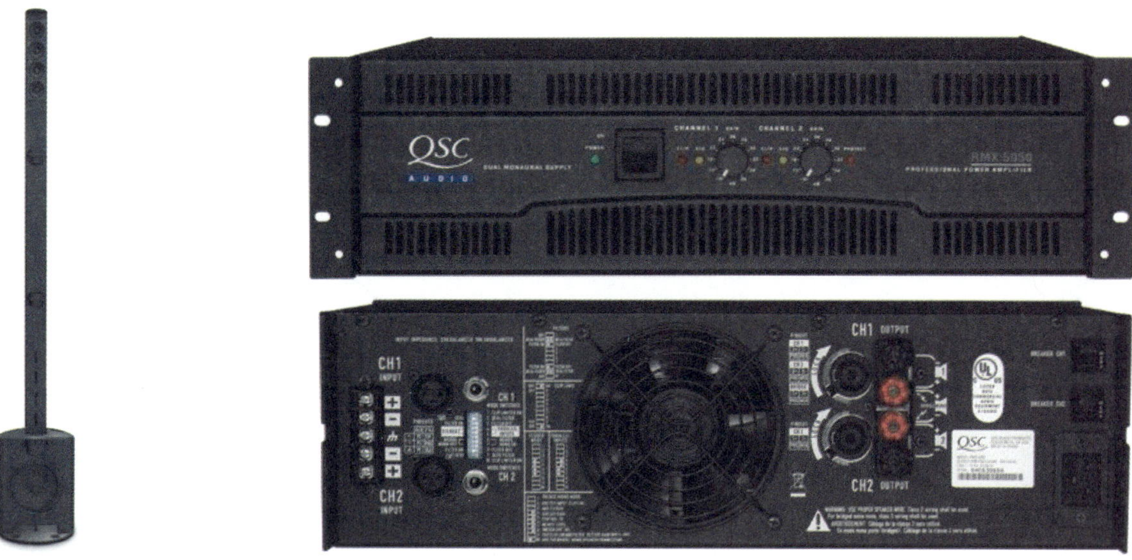

The image on the right shows the front and back of a powered amplifier for speakers that are passive. Most speakers that are commonly used for DJ setups today have built-in amplifiers, like the image to the left, but if you have passive speakers you'll need an amplifier.

WHERE are different types of speakers useful?

Portable speakers are great for mobile events where you're required to bring in your own equipment. Depending on the need, it's important to have enough coverage of the space. A lot of DJs make the mistake of buying very loud and powerful speakers that they then place incorrectly, making it incredibly loud near the speakers and hard to hear in the back of the room. (See Concept 12: Setting Up Speakers.)

HOW do I choose the right speaker?

Of course, budget is a determining factor in what you should buy. As with any other major purchase, it's important to do your own independent research but also ask for referrals. I would also recommend buying the additional insurance, especially with speakers. While you don't anticipate blowing a speaker, it does happen.

It's also important to think about how and when you would use your speakers. If you are just starting out, it may make more sense to rent speakers instead of owning them. Speakers can get expensive, and if you aren't gigging a lot, they may just be taking up space in your house. Also, technology continues to advance, and speakers get louder, get clearer, and have more features over time.

Related terms: active vs. passive, inputs, Bluetooth, sub vs. tops

CONCEPT 12:

Setting Up Speakers

WHAT are the first things I need to know about setting up speakers?
There are several things to consider when setting up. You'll want to be strategic about where to place the speakers and your DJ rig. If possible, avoid running cables across the room to prevent potential tripping hazards. Height is a huge factor that many times gets neglected. Make sure the speakers are at a height at which they can be heard. People, a wall, or any structure can get in the way of the sound and absorb it. Depending on your speakers, you may need speaker stands. Stands will raise the speakers to a height that will allow the music to travel and create more coverage. I have seen events where DJs placed speakers on the floor, and this is definitely not optimal. Distortion can also be a factor. Make sure to open the volume on your amp enough so there is less probability for distortion.

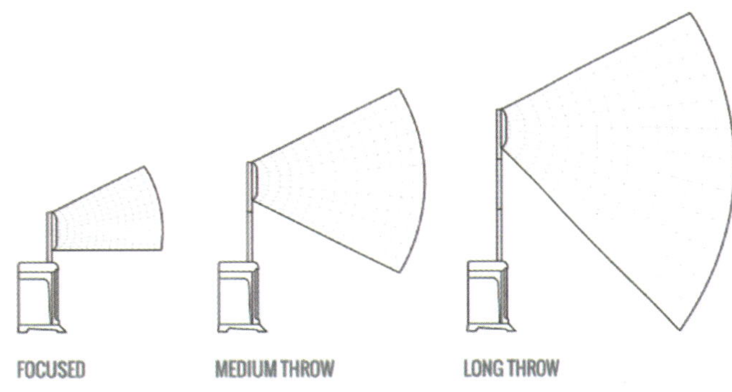

The height of the speaker is incredibly important and some speakers like the JBL Eon One have extra section lengths that can raise the speaker height to increase the throw.

WHY do I have to set up speakers properly?
This may be pretty obvious, but if your speakers aren't set up properly, you won't get the desired results at an event. An important concept to understand is coverage. It's imperative that you have enough coverage so that the music you are playing can be heard evenly throughout the room.

Allow yourself proper time to get set up and do a sound check. Your speakers will be set where they are, and it will be difficult to move them once the event is started. Also, keep in mind that the sound will be different once the space is filled with people, so be prepared to make slight volume adjustments once the event starts.

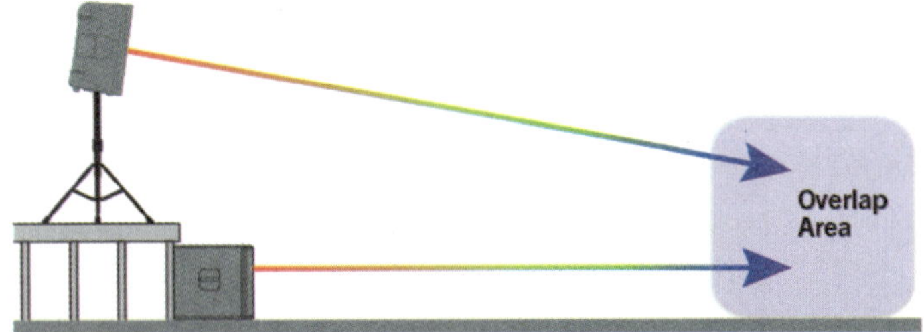

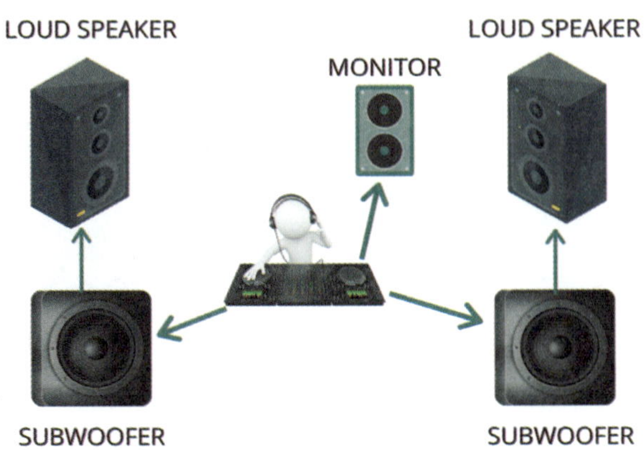

WHERE do I set the speakers?
Review your space and the number of speakers you have, then create a diagram of the elements to see where they should best be placed. This will help you achieve a balanced sound, depending on the dimensions or shape of the room. The placement depends on the number of speakers you have, because you'll want to ensure that

SMALL OUTDOOR

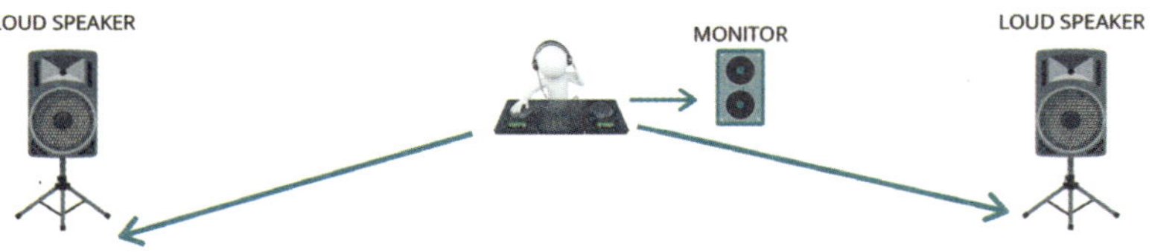

COCKTAIL TABLES

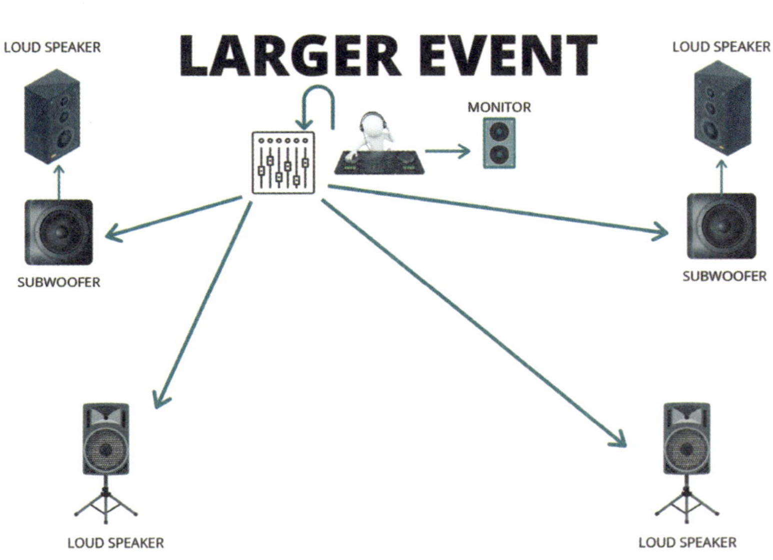

the sound travels and covers most of the space. This is also a great practice if you have additional hands and helpers with you. It will allow you to work more efficiently when you arrive, and will show that you have given thought to the setup and are a working professional.

HOW do I set up speakers properly?
Setting up the speakers properly is important to your DJ set and how it will sound for the audience. First, make sure the speakers are at the proper height, as mentioned earlier, so that the sound will travel freely through the space. Make sure to tape down the speaker cables to avoid accidents or obstruction. The aesthetics are just as important as the function. Taping down cables will help to make everything look polished and professional. It is an eyesore to have a bunch of cables running across the room instead of being neatly placed where they are supposed to be. In terms of tape, duct tape or painter's tape are not good ideas. Use professional gaffer's tape that will not leave a residue on the cables. This can be found at professional audio or video stores or online.

On the back of active speakers, there is sometimes a multi-convert input from the mic to the Line. You can put the XLR into it. Know the right setting you are plugging into if plugging the mic in directly, as the mic level input is different from the Line level input. To give you an idea of the difference, a Line level signal is 1 volt, or about 1,000 times as strong as a mic level signal. The two levels don't usually use the same input. This signal moves from your preamp to your amplifier. Remember also to start with the volume lower and raise it after you know you have a solid signal. This will prevent jarring and unwanted sounds to occur during a soundcheck and will also help prevent blowing a speaker.

Related terms: active vs. passive, inputs, Bluetooth, sub vs. tops

CONCEPT 13:

Choosing a Rig

WHAT DJ rig is best for me?

When learning to DJ, figuring out what DJ rig is best for you can be a daunting task. Budget is important to consider, and rest assured there are entry-level options available that are low cost but have a lot of features. This should be encouraging news. It is important not to buy the most expensive rig when getting started; at the same time, most people are not looking for something completely disposable.

Your goals as a DJ are a major factor in all this. There are two elements you use as a DJ: software and hardware. Most DJs make an initial commitment to software and then purchase corresponding hardware. If you are using Serato as your software, you have more options for equipment than other software with limited compatibility. For example, Native Instruments software, Traktor, is able to work only with Native Instruments hardware, which limits you to four options. However, if you are using Serato, there are about 50 different options for compatible hardware at various price points with various features.

Also, consider what you already have for equipment. Do you have a laptop? If so, it opens up options for you in the realm of software. If you have an iPad, it can be more limited. If you have a desktop, you can prep files, but it will likely be pretty inconvenient and impractical to carry a desktop computer to a gig. Create a list of what you already have and add to it what you think you might need.

< $500	$500 - $999	$1000 - $1999	> $2000
Very Portable	Portable	Semi-Portable	Not Easily Portable
All-in-One	All-in-One	All-in-One or Multiple Components	Multiple Components
1 USB	1 USB	Ability to Use 2 USBs	Ability to Use 2 USBs
USB Powered	Standalone Power	Standalone Power	Standalone Power
Consumer Grade Outputs	Pro Grade Outputs	Multiple Pro Grade Outputs	Multiple Pro Grade Outputs
Lite Version of Software	Pro Version of Software	Pro Version of Software	Pro Version of Software
Basic Features Accessible	Intermediate Features Accessible	Advanced Features Accessible	Advanced Features Accessible
Lowest Resale Value	Low Resale Value	Good Resale Value	Best Resale Value

WHY don't I just buy my favorite DJ's rig?

It's natural to want to use the rig that your favorite DJ uses. However, their rig might not fit your needs because your goals may be different from theirs. You will also hear statements being made in the music industry like "Real DJs use vinyl" and "CDJs are the best." It wasn't too long ago that I myself thought I would never use anything other than vinyl, but times change, technology progresses, and we evolve as artists as well. So try not to get too caught up in what others say or use. Look to those you trust for sound advice, read reviews about different equipment, and be honest with yourself about your budget and your realistic goals.

You'll also want to pay attention to the version of the equipment you are using. It can be difficult to work with outdated versions, particularly because there will be compatibility issues between hardware and software.

At the end of the day, there's a lot of truth in the statement that "it's not what you have, but how you use it." No matter what you are using, developing the fundamentals and skills to DJ will outweigh any equipment you have, no matter how expensive or feature-rich it may be. No matter what equipment you are using, the fundamental skills will always be necessary.

WHERE do I buy my rig?

DJ equipment is very specific, so it is important to get advice from salespeople who have a broad knowledge of different types across multiple manufacturers. A retail outlet that sells an assortment of equipment outside of the DJ field might not be the best place to get advice, as they might have a more general knowledge about what they are selling, rather than the kind of detailed information you need to make an informed decision.

It cannot be stressed enough that checking reviews written online or otherwise are helpful in determining what you need. Online reviews, which compare pros and cons, will help you see what type of equipment you need to achieve your goals. It would be helpful to test out the gear, but many online retailers have pretty good return policies in the event you are not fully satisfied.

When you are working from a limited budget, used equipment might seem like a logical solution—but be wary of this approach. Used equipment can often be outdated. Even if it's from a reputable brand, it might be an older version that is not compatible with the updated software you use.

HOW do I get the most out of my budget?

Think through your goals before searching for what you need. Consult people you trust and who are unbiased—and preferably not paid on a commission basis. It's not that you shouldn't purchase from someone who gets a commission, as you will not always know their compensation structure; and it's not to say that those who make a commission cannot be truthful. The point here is to make sure you speak with someone who is trying to educate you and is interested in pointing you toward what you need rather than pushing the most expensive product.

You don't always want the cheapest or the most basic product. It's not always better to have more features, but you will likely want the ability to grow with your equipment as your skills grow. Also, the cheaper the DJ equipment, the more likely it will not retain its value if you decide to sell it on the used market when you want to upgrade.

Related terms: equipment, CDJs, turntables, controllers, mixers, all-in-one, software

CONCEPT 14:
Choosing DJ Software

WHAT DJ software is best for me?

Today, software is more important than the hardware. It is what powers your system. Most people stick to the same software, so it's good to decide on what you want to use for semi-long term. It doesn't have to be the only software you will ever use, but most DJs end up sticking with the same programs for years and find that switching can be cumbersome.

SERATO DJ PRO	REKORDBOX	TRAKTOR PRO 3
Works with many different controllers and mixers	Works with Pioneer DJ specific hardware	Works with Native Instruments specific hardware + CDJs
Easy to use interface	Complicated user interface	Fairly complicated user interface
Free with select hardware or can be purchased	Free software, upgrade for a fee	Free software
Streaming Services: Tidal, Soundcloud Go+	Streaming Services: Soundcloud Go+, Beatport Link, Beatsource	Streaming Services: none yet
Expansion Packs including Video for purchase	Lighting, Lyrics, and Video Modes	Stem and Remix Decks

DJAY	WEDJ	TRAKTOR DJ 2
Works with many different controllers and mixers	Works with Pioneer DJ specific hardware	Works with Native Instruments specific hardware
Easy to use interface	Fairly complicated user interface	Fairly complicated user interface
Free with monthly subscription	Free	Free
Streaming Services: Tidal, Soundcloud Go+, Beatport Link, Beatsource	Streaming Services: Soundcloud Go+, Beatport Link, Beatsource	Streaming Services: Soundcloud Go+
Expansion Packs including Sampler, Video, 4 Decks	Phrase Detection great for learning	Auto-Save Collection

For most DJ software, there are free versions you can get. Some examples of this include Virtual DJ, rekordbox, and Serato DJ Lite. While there are quite a few options out there, I would consider Serato, rekordbox, Traktor, Hercules's DJUCED, and Virtual DJ. Like most software in other industries, all of these programs have similar features with some differences in layout (user interface), intermediate to advanced features, and compatibility with hardware.

WHY don't I just use my favorite DJ's software?

A lot of DJs learn by watching other people. If you know a DJ and they seem happy with their software, you might be prone to use the same; however, this is not always the best way to make a purchase. Purchasing a car is a good example. Just because a friend bought a car they are happy with doesn't mean that the same car is going to meet your needs.

Sometimes the difference between software programs is minimal. Once you know a program, transitioning to another is not difficult—if you are open to it. Be mindful of the fact that software gets updated regularly and staying on top of that is important. As a DJ in the modern era, you will be forced to become fairly tech savvy and learn terms like "firmware," "drivers," and "compatible operating system."

WHERE do I buy software?

Most hardware is built to work with some form of software. You can visit a company's website to learn more about the compatibility. Most times, you can even download the software without having the controller. This can be a great way to test out the software before committing to more expensive hardware.

HOW do I choose?

Think about the goals you have outlined for yourself and try to align your software purchase with those goals. You'll want room to grow with your DJing skills and what you use to perform. Some software programs include other features that go beyond DJing. For instance, rekordbox and Serato have a video DJing component, or the ability to control lighting. Traktor has remix decks, all of which go beyond the art of basic DJing.

Keep in mind that even after committing to a software program, it is possible to make a switch. Migrating your music library is the hardest part, but there are a few third-party apps to help you do that. One of the biggest fears for DJs is losing music in the process of migrating playlists. Find software that you like and that is easy to understand—and just keep in mind that as you are learning the fundamentals with one software, almost all of those skills will transfer to another software.

Related terms: equipment, CDJs, turntables, controllers, mixers, all-in-one, Serato, Traktor, rekordbox, DJUCED, djay, Engine Prime, Virtual DJ

CONCEPT 15:
Getting Music

WHAT kind of music should I get?
Without music, your DJ equipment is virtually useless. Unlike other instruments used to compose music, a DJ rig needs music in the same way a car needs fuel. The music you accumulate will determine your "sound" as a DJ as you mix it all together.

PURCHASE PER TRACK	MONTHLY DUES	STREAMING
iTunes	BPM Supreme	TIDAL
Amazon Music	Headliner Record Pool	Soundcloud Go+
Google Play Music	Direct Music Service	Beatport Link
Beatport	My MP3 Pool	Beatsource Link
Beatsource	Promo Only	Qobuz

At the time of writing this, DJs still need to download music as MP3s or WAV files, although streaming is starting to become integrated into many different brands of software. Streaming is available, but it's still not very reliable in a live environment, as there are challenges with Wi-Fi strength.

When first learning, it is extremely helpful for the development of your craft to find friendly edits and versions of songs. These alternative versions of songs are usually noted as being shortened or extended. They tend to be easier to perform with and will help with your mixing.

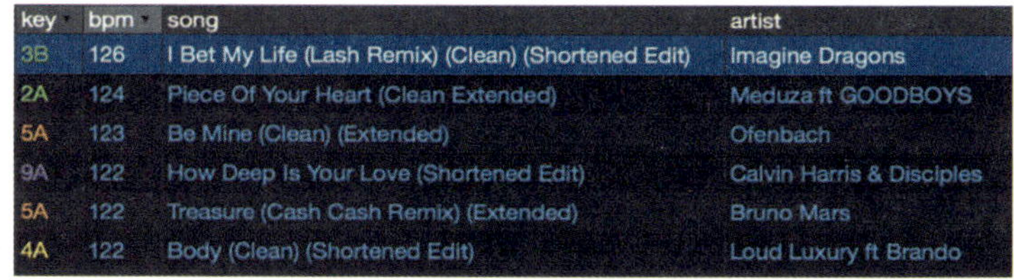

key	bpm	song	artist
3B	126	I Bet My Life (Lash Remix) (Clean) (Shortened Edit)	Imagine Dragons
2A	124	Piece Of Your Heart (Clean Extended)	Meduza ft GOODBOYS
5A	123	Be Mine (Clean) (Extended)	Ofenbach
9A	122	How Deep Is Your Love (Shortened Edit)	Calvin Harris & Disciples
5A	122	Treasure (Cash Cash Remix) (Extended)	Bruno Mars
4A	122	Body (Clean) (Shortened Edit)	Loud Luxury ft Brando

Also, consider the file types for your music. MP3s are compressed audio files, and not all MP3s are created equally. These files are dependent on bit rate. The bit rate on the low end is 96, which means the file is *compressed*; in other words, the high-high frequencies and the low-low frequencies have been taken out, leaving you what's in the middle. The result is that when you play on a robust system, it will feel sort of empty and will not hit as hard or be as full sounding as you might desire.

A WAV file is 6 to 10 times the size of an MP3. It is raw audio, so it is higher quality. This means it will take up much more space on your hard drive. Unfortunately, depending on the music you are looking for, raw WAV files may not be available.

As a DJ, you are likely not collecting albums in their entirety to add to your DJ library. You may still download and collect albums as a listener, but it's important to start separating your "consumer library" from your "DJ library."

WHY should I use a record pool?
A digital DJ *record pool* is a subscription site that provides specific DJ-ready MP3s to download and add to your library. Most record pools are platforms that have been built for DJs by DJs. The service allows DJs who pay a monthly subscription fee to download current popular songs. Typically, these are high-quality MP3s of extended and shortened versions for easier mixing. Record pools cater to mobile and to club DJs. They are really great resources for the professional DJ.

WISHLIST

BROWSE
- NEW RELEASES
- EXCLUSIVES
- CUSTOM SEARCH
- TOP DOWNLOADS
- DECADES ▸

YEAR GO

GENRES
- POP
- HIP HOP
- R&B
- HOUSE/EDM
- ROCK/ALT
- INDIE/NEW WAVE
- DISCO/FUNK
- REGGAE
- COUNTRY
- DJ TOOLS ▸

ADDED ▾	YEAR	ARTIST	TITLE	EDITOR	BPM	ACTION
6 / 12 / 2020	2020	Lil Wayne ft Doja Cat	Shimmy (DJ Rocco & DJ Ever B Remix / Dirty)	DMS	99	
6 / 12 / 2020	2020	Lil Wayne ft Doja Cat	Shimmy (PeteDown Hype Clap Intro / Clean)	DMS	98	
6 / 12 / 2020	2020	Lil Wayne ft Doja Cat	Shimmy (PeteDown Hype Clap Intro / Dirty)	DMS	98	
6 / 12 / 2020	2020	Jack Harlow	Whats Poppin (Transition 95-73 / Clean)	PeteDown	95	
6 / 12 / 2020	2020	Jack Harlow	Whats Poppin (Transition 95-73 / Dirty)	PeteDown	95	
6 / 12 / 2020	2020	Katy Perry vs Faul Wad	Teenage Dream In Tokyo (Fuseamania Bootleg)	Fuseamania	125	
6 / 12 / 2020	2020	Katy Perry vs Faul Wad	Teenage Dream In Tokyo (Fuseamania Bootleg / Short Edit)	Fuseamania	125	
6 / 12 / 2020	2020	Lady Gaga & Ariana Grande	Rain On Me (Jose Knight Remix)	DMS	124	
6 / 12 / 2020	2020	CID ft Jaquell	Downstairs	DMS	126	
6 / 12 / 2020	1984	Depeche Mode	Blasphemous Rumours (Dominatrix RMX / Cutdown)	Jason Bee	119	
6 / 12 / 2020	1987	Depeche Mode	Never Let Me Down Again (Retro Shock RMX / Cutdown)	DMS	106	
6 / 12 / 2020	1992	House Of Pain	Jump Around (Flat Intro)	Simo	107	
6 / 12 / 2020	1992	House Of Pain	Jump Around (Flat Intro / Short Edit)	Simo	107	
6 / 12 / 2020	1992	House Of Pain	Jump Around (Flat Intro / Super Short Edit)	Simo	107	
6 / 12 / 2020	1989	Queen Latifah ft Monie Love	Ladies First	Simo	107	
6 / 12 / 2020	1989	Queen Latifah ft Monie Love	Ladies First (Super Short Edit)	Simo	107	
6 / 12 / 2020	1989	Queen Latifah ft Monie Love	Ladies First (45 King Remix)	DMS	108	
6 / 12 / 2020	1989	Queen Latifah ft Monie Love	Ladies First (45 King RMX / Short Edit)	DMS	108	
6 / 11 / 2020	1993	The Pharcyde	Passin' Me By (Clean)	Simo	87	
6 / 11 / 2020	1993	The Pharcyde	Passin' Me By (Clean / Short Edit)	Simo	87	

WHERE do I get music?

Since not all the music you need or want will be found exclusively in one place, it is part of DJ culture to be willing and enthusiastic about "digging" for music.

There are many places online where you can purchase music. Per-song avenues include iTunes, Google Play, Amazon, and Beatport. There are streaming services you can subscribe to such as Spotify, Tidal, and SoundCloud. Plus, the record pool option mentioned earlier is great for providing DJ-friendly song versions through a monthly subscription.

Beyond that, there is the option of digging through vinyl, CDs, and even cassettes to find different songs and samples to import into your library.

HOW do I use music I already own?

Just as you will want to go through the DJ equipment you already own—to see if it meets your needs and you're able to build on it to ultimately meet your goals—you'll want to go through the music you already own. Make sure to check the bit rate because you have likely accumulated music over the years and never needed to worry, as a general listener, about the quality of the files. You can import these songs into your library by simply dragging and dropping into the DJ software. Most DJ software is also able to read iTunes; however, if all your general listening music is stored and being organized in iTunes, I recommend keeping your DJ library in your DJ software. That way you can keep the two music collections separate.

Related terms: iTunes, Amazon, Beatport, record pools, streaming

CONCEPT 16:
Analyzing Files

WHAT is analyzing files?
Your software uses an algorithm to identify the BPM, key, and beat grid, and to build a waveform view.

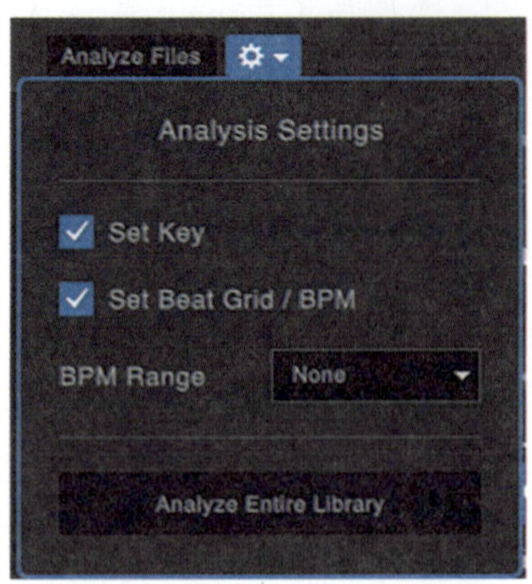

WHY should I analyze files?
You should analyze your files in the preparation phase, before you perform. In certain programs, you cannot analyze while playing live. The analysis requires a good amount of processing power from your computer's CPU, so this would affect its performance and cause glitching issues.

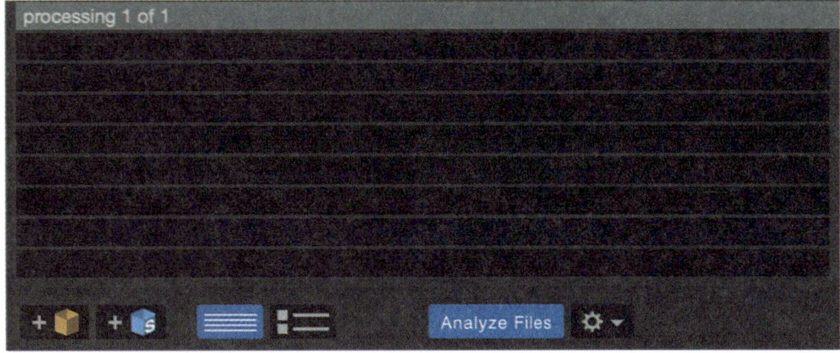

Analyzing the files will give you more information about the songs you are playing. You could try to guess the BPM or key, but this approach is definitely not optimal; it is much more helpful to fully understand the songs you are playing so you can decide which songs are compatible with one another.

WHERE is the analysis stored?
Depending on your software, your files can be stored differently. Some software has a separate database for your files, which is usually found inside a folder named after the software inside either your Music or Documents folder.

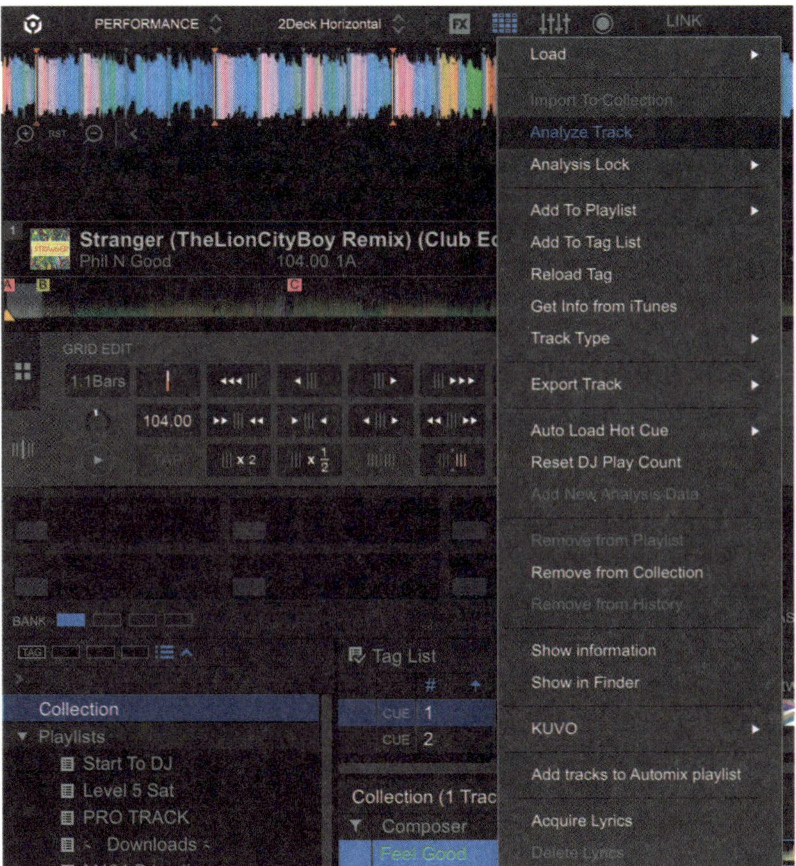

Other programs store this information to the MP3 tag of the file itself. Generally, I prefer this because the information travels with the MP3 file. This is particularly helpful if you have multiple computers or are sharing files with other people. For example, if I have a song stored in Serato and it has Hot Cues, loops, and particular notes on the track, I can send this MP3 to you and you would see all of that information as soon as you load the song into your Serato software.

HOW do I analyze?

Analyzing comes down to how much memory your laptop has and how much load it can handle. You can usually drag and drop individual folders to analyze specific groups of files at a time. Once you've analyzed your file, you can sort by BPM or by key. Specifically for Serato users, you will work with your files in offline mode.

Typically, when you load a song onto one of the decks, your software will start to analyze the file; however, I would not recommend this as your primary way to analyze files. In most DJ software, you will have the option to either analyze each track individually or batch analyze.

With individual analysis, right-click (or Command-click) on the file inside the browser of your DJ software. This will likely bring up some options, and one of them will be to analyze the file. Some programs will ask you to check off what parameters you want to include in the analysis. By default, BPM and beat grid are the most necessary. Some DJs like to use third-party applications for key analysis due to accuracy issues (see Concept 27: Key/Key Lock and Concept 28: Harmonic Mixing).

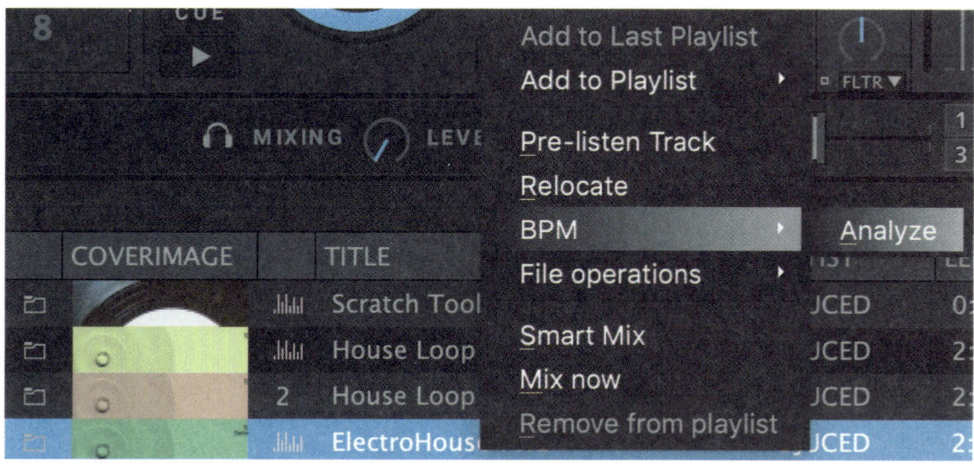

Most DJ software will allow you to "batch analyze," which can be helpful—but will also put more load on your computer. I recommend doing any batch analysis overnight.

Related terms: MP3, Serato, rekordbox, Traktor, DJUCED, djay, Engine Prime

CONCEPT 17:
Editing Grids

WHAT is the grid?

A *beat grid* (or *beatgrid* in Serato) is a series of markers that point to the location of beats within the track's waveform. Beat grids are used for advanced mixing functions such as track Sync, precise effects synchronization, looping, and accurate BPM representation.

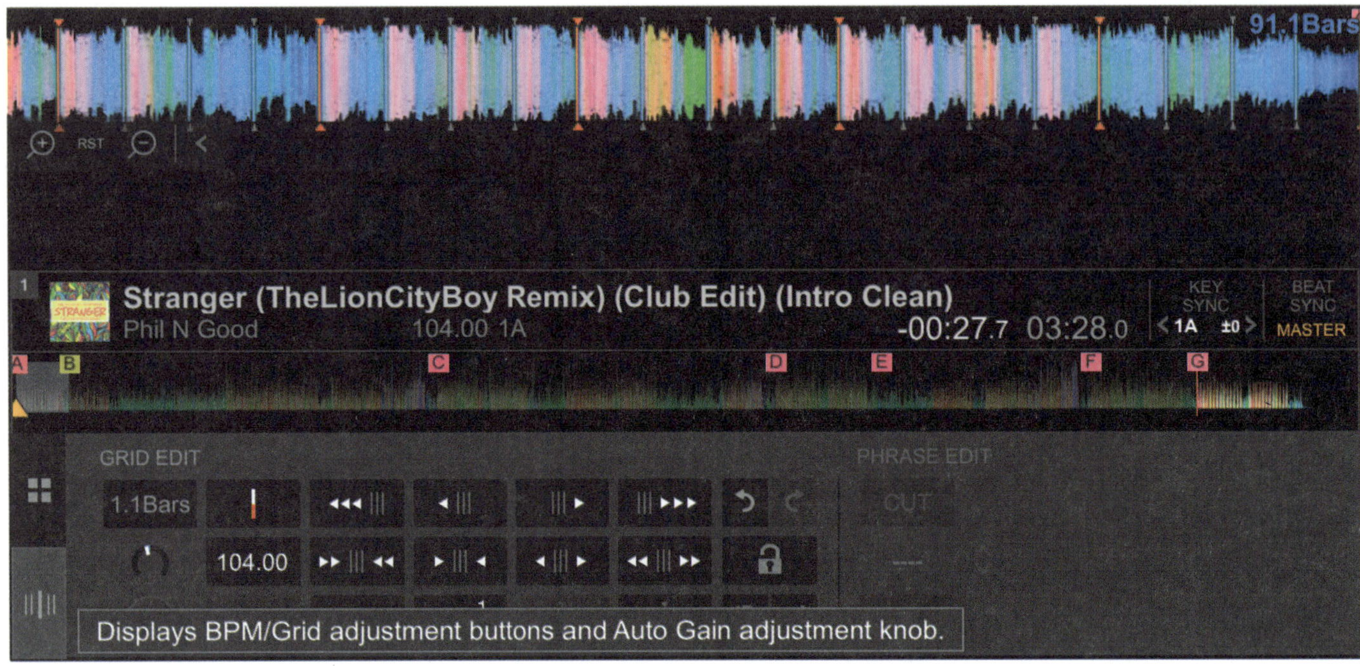

The grid visually depicts each beat of the track with a vertical line.

WHY is the grid important?

The grid is important for syncing. If you are trying to sync up two tracks and the beat grid is wrong, it will sound like horses galloping, or shoes in the dryer. Often, when I listen to my students' mixes and the beats are off, I can predict that their beat grids are off. This can be incredibly frustrating and confusing for beginners, especially after assuming their song choices would mix well with each other.

The same is true with setting an auto-loop that follows the beat grid. If the beat grid is wrong, the loop will sound off. For instance, if you set a 2-beat loop, but your beat grid is off, it will sound longer or shorter than the 2 beats. This will dramatically throw off your mixing. Here's an analogy: If you measure a room for new carpeting and your measurement is off, the carpet will either be too big or too small for the room, and ultimately will not fit.

The beat grid is important for rhythm-based effects as well, as they rely on it to properly create the effect you want during your performance.

WHERE do I find the grid?

Once the waveform has been loaded on the deck, you should see the beat grid as soon as it has been created. In some software, you can toggle the beat grid on and off, so make sure that you have it checked on in your preferences. Most beat grids will also display some form of musical bar or beat count that can be helpful when trying to figure out phrase lengths.

Software with beat grid turned off

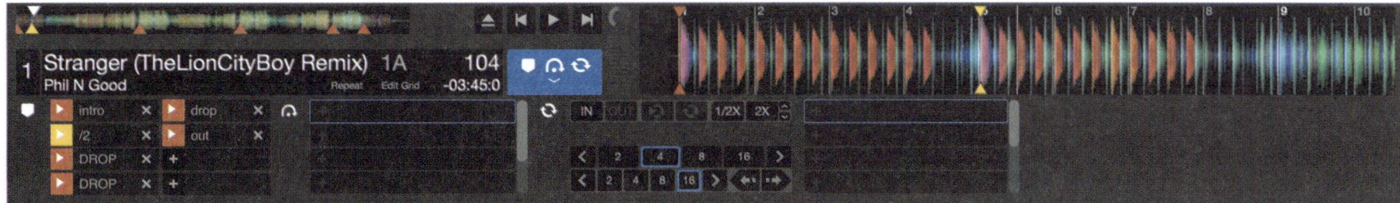

Software with beat grid turned on

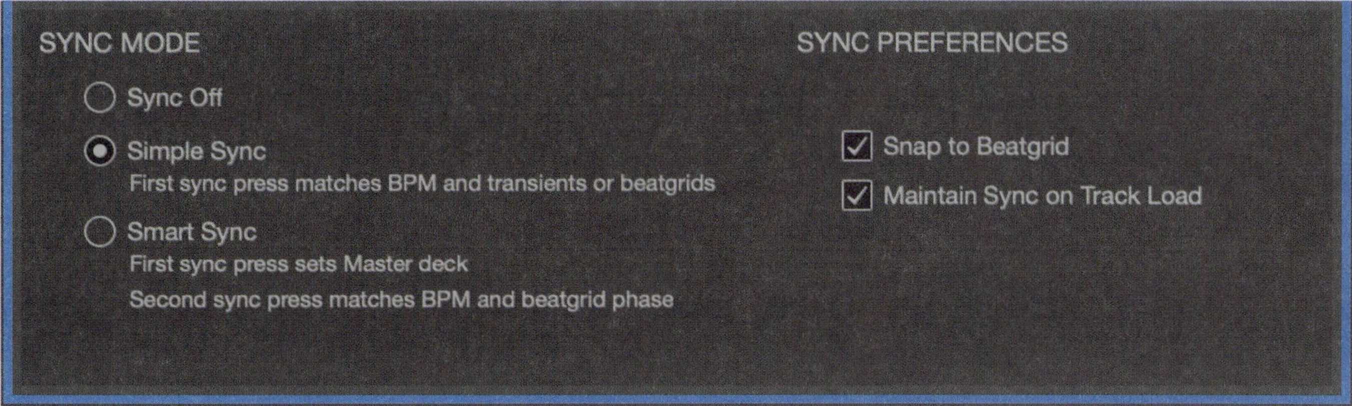

HOW do I edit the grid?

You'll want to become familiar with editing the grid, and there are several ways to do this based on what is wrong.

First of all, make sure the BPM is correct in your DJ software. It's very possible that the software may have gotten the BPM wrong when the song was being analyzed. While the software is fairly accurate, it's not 100% accurate, as it's using an algorithm to compute the tempo. The algorithm can get confused by different rhythms or acapella sections of a track that do not have a beat.

You can use a beat counter to help you find the BPM by tapping in the tempo. There are free mobile apps that can help with this, and I highly recommend downloading one. Not only can this help with figuring out a song in your library, but it can also be used as a tool when listening to songs on the radio.

Once you have figured out the right BPM, you will need to reset the grid. Most of the time, this will fix the issue. In the event it doesn't, you may have a situation in which the tempo changes within the song or the song was created with a live drummer. In a case like this, you will need to mix the song in without a proper beat grid, and this is when learning how to manually beatmatch is incredibly important.

In some cases, when a song is analyzed, the software sets the beat grid on a sound other than the first downbeat. The grid itself is correct and set to the correct BPM, but the grid needs to be "shifted" to either the right or the left.

Related terms: BPM, tempo, adjust, slip, setting the 1, changing BPM

CONCEPT 18:

Cues

WHAT are cues?

TEMPORARY CUE	HOT CUE	MEMORY CUE
Only 1	3 to 8	10
On all DJ gear	On all DJ gear	On rekordbox gear
Temporary	Saved to track or database	Saved to track or database
Usually white or orange	Can be colored	Usually red
Can use a specific button to trigger "cue"	Can use a specific performance pad or button to trigger	Need to use the "call" button to find the cue you want
Primarily used to "cue" up to a section before playing it	Primarily used to jump to a point in the song	Primarily used to "bookmark" a part in a song

In general, a *cue* is a marker that we set and use to trigger a particular part of a song when we are playing music. I like to think of a cue as a bookmark. There are different types of cues, and each of them has different behaviors and uses. The most common cues are *Hot Cues* and *temporary cues*.

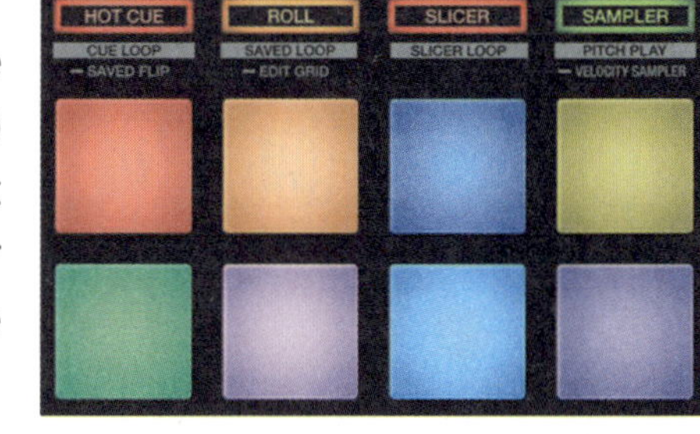

Hot Cues usually correspond to performance pads on the controller or mixer. They can change color (in some software) and are saved to the file or database. When you trigger a Hot Cue, no matter where you are in the song, it will jump back or forward to where that Hot Cue is. Most DJ software will have anywhere from three to eight Hot Cues.

A temporary cue will change depending on when you set it, and most DJ software gives you one temporary cue. This is typically used for jumping back to the beginning of the song but can be moved to any desired position. As the name states, this cue is temporary, so when you load that song the next time, the temporary cue will be gone.

WHY are cues useful?

Cues help to separate a song and also allow the DJ to be creative. A DJ can rearrange a song live by playing the intro and then using a Hot Cue to jump directly to the final chorus. Hot Cues can also be used to replay a section of a song or even a particular word or phrase in the song. This can be used to create a "stutter" effect or can even be used to create a beat live by playing a drum sample.

In the past, with a vinyl record, a DJ couldn't use a Hot Cue and jump to different sections of a song. Many DJs today have not had the experience of having to lift a needle up and place it in the right spot. It is very difficult to do and requires a lot of practice.

Hot Cues can also be used to help visualize the different sections or phrases of a song. This is a great way to start thinking of music as a collection of different sections that can be used creatively instead of simply treating the song as a finalized, completed piece of music.

WHERE should I set cues?

The most important place that I set a cue is at the beginning of the first downbeat, otherwise known as the "1." This allows the DJ to be able to quickly jump back to the beginning of the song when preparing to mix songs together live. Often, I am auditioning songs in my headphones before bringing them in live, and the first cue (whether Hot Cue or temporary cue) saves a lot of time getting back to the beginning of the intro when mixing the song in.

You can also set cues at any point of interest. These are usually the chorus or where you plan to mix out of the song. Other useful places to set Hot Cues are at the beginning of an acapella section, breakdown, or outro. Ultimately, it's up to you how and where you use Hot Cues. I would also recommend not creating too many cues on a song. This would be the equivalent of highlighting an entire page of text. The highlighted section should stand out and help jog your memory.

HOW do I set, store, and change cues?

A helpful way to set your cues is to learn keyboard shortcuts in your DJ software. I am often setting Hot Cues with just my laptop, with no controller or DJ equipment plugged in, so learning the computer keyboard shortcuts is very helpful for working more efficiently. You can also use your DJ controller for setting Hot Cues, but I recommend learning the keyboard commands so you don't have to pull out the controller every time you want to prepare your files.

It's also important to know how to change or delete Hot Cues. Most Hot Cues will have a small "x" next to them and clicking on that will delete the Hot Cue. On the controller, a universal command is to hold the shift button and hit the Hot Cue that you wish to delete.

Related terms: Hot Cues, memory cues, temporary cues

CONCEPT 19:

Hot Cue Strategy

WHAT is the Hot Cue strategy?

The main concept behind this strategy is to use Hot Cues to break up a song and better understand its structure. This will help you mix better as a DJ. The idea is to use Hot Cues to mark "In" and "Out" points in a track and to change the hot cue color to denote the length of those sections. (Note: This is available in some but not all DJ software programs.)

WHY use this strategy?

I started using this strategy several years ago in my own library, but it stemmed from a conversation I was having with a student of mine. He was asking me what the colors meant for the different Hot Cues. At the time, I hadn't changed the colors of the Hot Cues to signify anything, they were just the default colors. A lightbulb went off in my head. This was an opportunity to give Hot Cues more significance—something that would be extremely helpful when glancing at a song in the software. I started to create a system for the colors (yellow = 4 bars, red = 8 bars, etc.). This made it so much easier to mix and to teach other people where to mix.

For instance, if the chorus of Song A is 8 bars and has a red Hot Cue at the beginning, and the intro of Song B is also 8 bars and also has a red Hot Cue at the beginning, then you're simply lining up the colors!

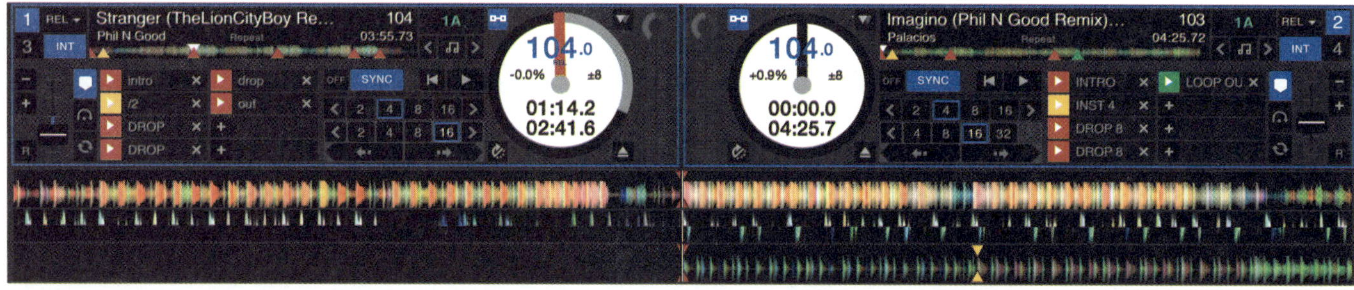

WHERE should I set cues?

Your primary Hot Cues are for getting in and out. Those are the important ones, especially if you are using software that has limitations. If you have other ideas for Hot Cues, you would add them in after setting the primary ones.

Set the Hot Cues at the most important places to get in and out, like the 1st chorus and 2nd chorus. It's helpful to set the Hot Cue at the beginning of the section you want to get out on. I know some people set the Hot Cue at the end of the phrase, but I find that still doesn't give me a good idea of the length of the section and where to line up the next song.

Most DJ software maxes out at eight Hot Cues, and to be honest, you don't need more than that. Be wary of "over-Hot Cueing," as this will defeat the purpose of being able to break up the song. In the songs in my library, I typically have two Hot Cues reserved for ways to get in (usually at the "1" of the intro and maybe a second point halfway through the intro), and the rest I save for ways to get out. I usually use only four to five Hot Cues per song.

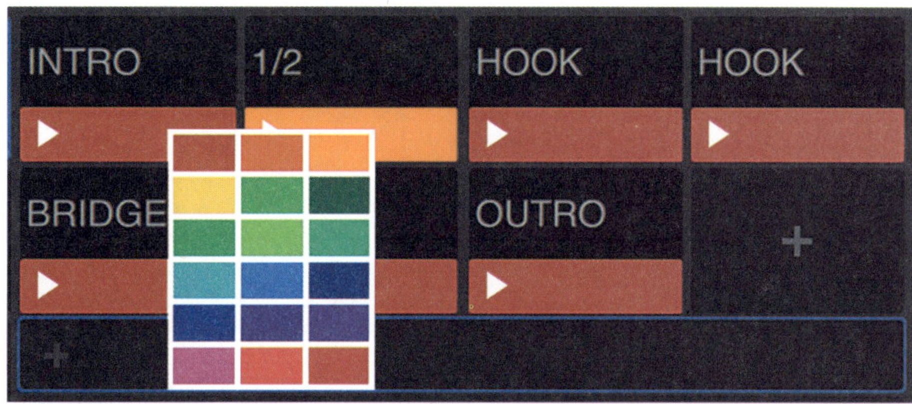

You can change the color of a Hot Cue by right-clicking or Command-clicking (Mac) on the Hot Cue itself in the software. Some DJ software also allows you to write a note on the Hot Cue, which is really helpful.

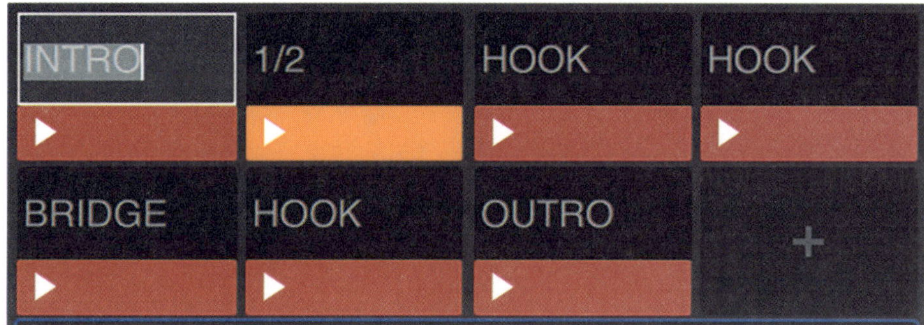

HOW do I implement?

The first thing you need to do is figure out the song. I call this "mapping out the song" (see Concept 3: Mapping Out Songs). Once you figure out the lengths of the sections of interest (intro, chorus, drop, other mixpoints), you can then begin to allocate your Hot Cues.

Make sure you zoom into the waveform before setting a Hot Cue so that you know for certain you are right on the beat. This will be really important when you are trying to jump back to the section. If there is a little bit of space between the Hot Cue and the actual beat, your timing will be off. If for some reason you set the Hot Cue and it's not exactly on the beat when you zoom in, you will have to delete that point and reset it.

There's also a Quantize feature that can help you set these Hot Cues quickly and accurately on the grid.

Once you set your Hot Cues, go in and change the color by right-clicking on the Hot Cue and selecting the color you want. You are more than welcome to adopt my colors, or you can create your own system!

Related terms: colors, labels, mapping out songs

CONCEPT 20:

Reading the Waveform

WHAT is the waveform?

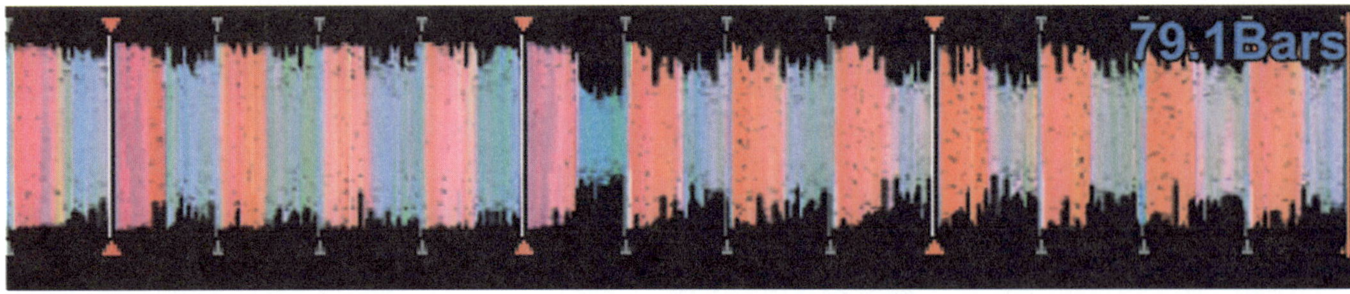

The waveform is the real-time visual representation of the sonic action in a track. In the waveform, you can see the peaks and valleys depicting the louder and softer parts of the song.

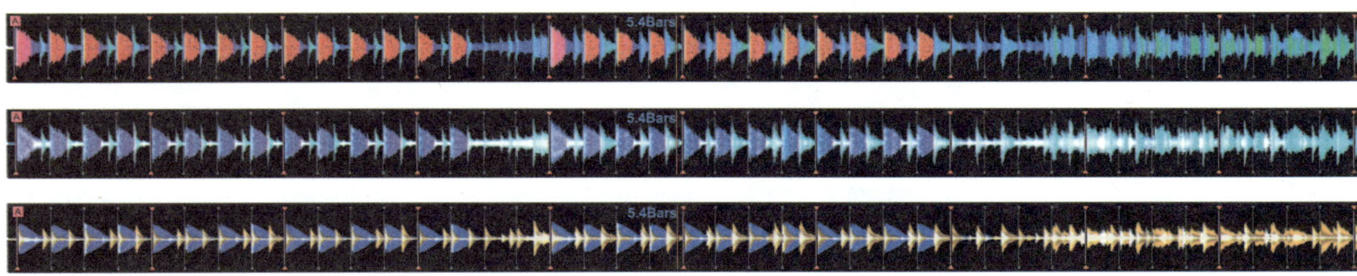

WHY is the waveform important?

The waveform allows you to see how a song changes over time. For instance, if you look down the waveform preview, you can see where there might be a dip in the music during a breakdown, or when the beat comes back in. All these visual cues will help you better understand what is happening in the music.

Zooming into the waveform allows you to set the Hot Cues accurately. By doing this, you can see where to set the marks and also ensure the grid is correct.

Some software programs are designed so that the color is in RBG mode. In this case, you can tell what's going on easily by just looking at the colors. If you remove certain frequencies by eliminating them with the EQ knob, you are also removing their corresponding colors. For instance, if you remove the low end, you would also remove the red color, and the waveform display will be mostly green and blue. If you remove the mid frequencies, the green will be eliminated, and the waveform will be mostly blue and red. Finally, by removing the high-end frequencies, the blue will be eliminated, and the waveform will be mostly red and green. When a waveform shows a section that lacks red, that part of the song probably lacks drums and bass.

Red depicts a low frequency and is more prominent in an EDM, bass-driven song. Green, however, shows the mid-range frequencies and tends to be prominent in sections without drums.

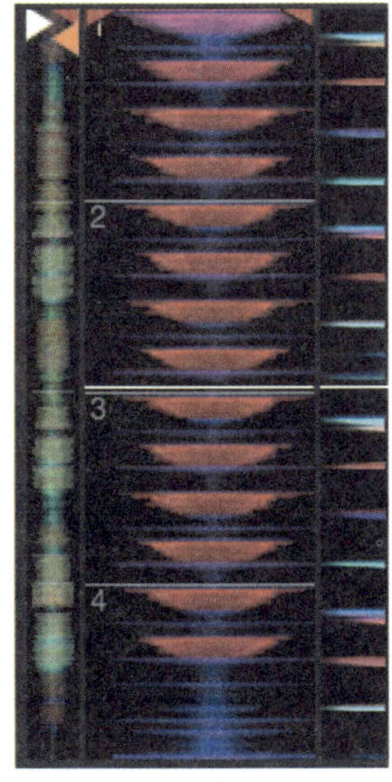

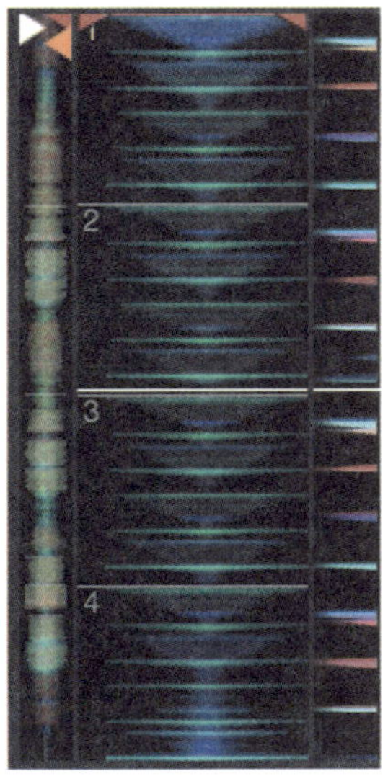

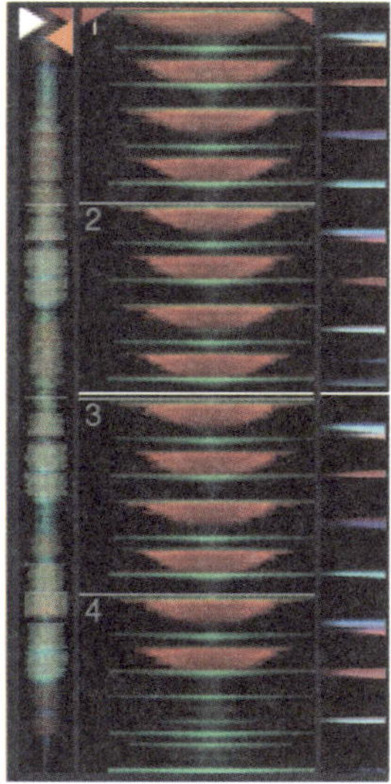

WHERE do I find the waveform?

You will find the waveforms in the DJ software, although they are displayed in some hardware as well.

Keep in mind, it's not suitable to watch the waveforms while DJing. It's meant to be more of a reference, as there is a slight delay between what you are seeing in the waveform and what is actually happening. My advice is to avoid getting in the habit of screen watching or focusing on the waveform. You may be practicing at home without an audience, but once you are in front of an audience, this tip becomes more important—nobody wants to watch a performer who is staring at a screen.

Another tip is to situate your laptop off to your side as opposed to right in front of you in your eyeline. This has dramatically helped me to avoid getting "sucked" into my screen while DJing. Instead, I am able to focus on the audience, observing and connecting with the dancefloor.

HOW do I look at a waveform?

It's really important to learn how to zoom in and out of the waveform. Depending on your DJ software, there are different keyboard shortcuts for this. Most software uses some combination of the "-" and "+" buttons on your laptop keyboard.

Zooming in and out is essential for setting Hot Cues and making sure they are accurate. However, during your performance, it's best only to glance at the waveform and zoom out a bit. This way you are not focused on it and can see further into the future of the song if needed.

It's also good to note that there is no waveform on vinyl. Sometimes people develop a crutch, thinking that watching the waveforms will help them match the beats better, but this is not the case. Start to develop your listening skills and go by what you hear instead of what you see. Remember, music is heard, not seen. The waveform is only a visual representation, so you should put more emphasis on what you are hearing and the rhythms your body is moving to.

Related terms: colors, size, zoom, grid

CONCEPT 21:

Extending Intros

WHAT is extending intros?

Extending an intro is when you lengthen the instrumental introduction of a song in order to layer it underneath the chorus of another song. If we are going to mix two songs together, we would mix out at a high point, such as a chorus, where you may already have vocals. You want to avoid having vocals over more vocals because this is very jarring to the audience. Imagine listening to two people tell you a story at the same time. Which one are you listening to? It's almost impossible to focus on both at the same time.

What you are looking for in the song coming in is an instrumental intro that is ideally at least 4, 8, or 16 bars long. This can be a bit of an issue when first starting off, as most of the songs in your listening library likely won't have these extended intros. As a listener, the extended instrumental section doesn't usually have a purpose, but as a DJ, it can be super helpful when mixing two songs together.

If you were to produce a song today that you want DJs to play for their dancefloors, you would want to make an extended version of the song. Extended versions aren't usually found on platforms like Spotify or iTunes. Most of these versions are found on DJ-specific websites (digital record pools), or DJs will make these edits themselves and share with fellow DJs.

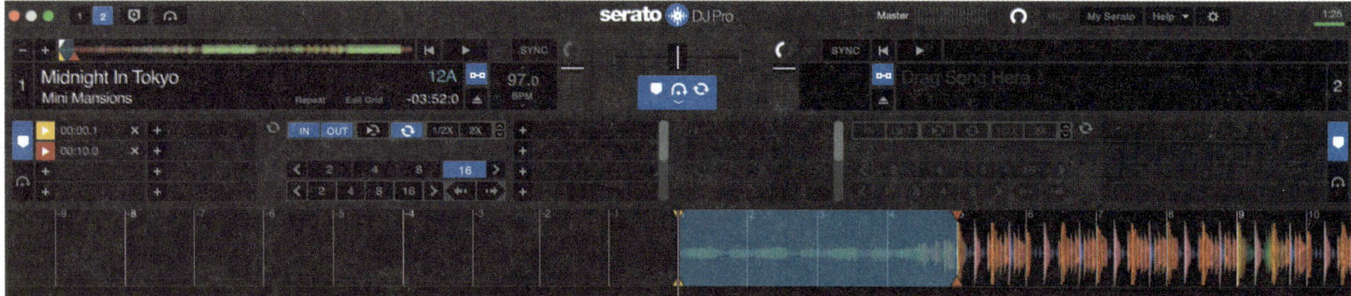

WHY is extending an intro important?

As you mix from one song to the next, you can lay the extended intro underneath the current song that the audience is listening or dancing to. As you begin to increase the volume of the intro, the audience is given an audible cue that something is going to change because the current song is being blended with the new beat of the song that is coming up.

The transition feels seamless because of the extended intro beneath the current song. As a listener, you're focused on the chorus, but the new beat is creating a seamless blend into another song. This is one of the magical parts of DJing! It's the concept of playing two songs at the same time and finding a way to smoothly transition between the two without any pause or abrupt stop.

When trying to manage the energy of a dancefloor, this seamless blending is very important. It keeps the audience dancing at a steady tempo and allows for no drop-off in energy as you transition between the songs.

WHERE do I extend an intro?

In the digital era of DJing, there are quite a few tools to help you extend an intro. First, identify whether you already have an instrumental section at the beginning of the song. This would be done before playing live. If you have an instrumental intro already, how long is it? Is it longer than 4 bars? If it's not, you may want to extend the intro. You can do this by setting a loop in your DJ software.

Let's say you have a 4-bar instrumental section at the beginning of the song. Four bars is the same as 16 beats. In your DJ software, you would set a 16-beat loop starting at the beginning of the instrumental section and ending at the end of it. Once you activate the loop, the track will repeat that section indefinitely until you release it. This can now be layered underneath the song you are mixing out of. When you release the loop depends on the length of the other song's section that you are trying to mix out of.

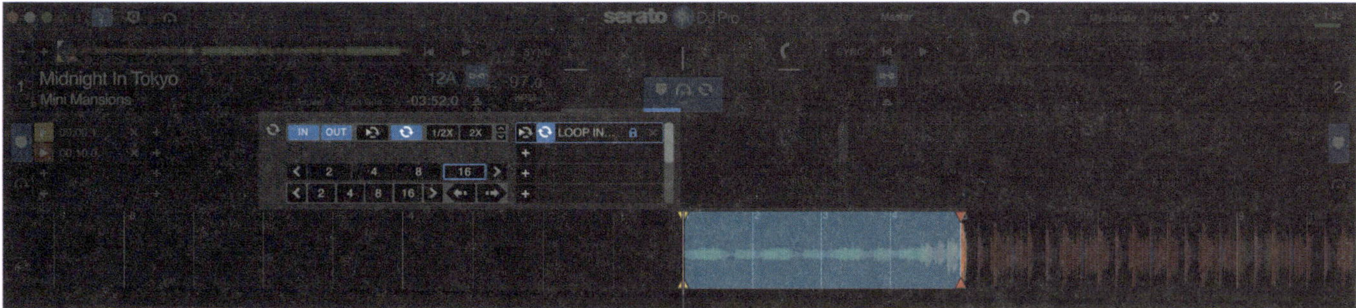

If for some reason there is no instrumental section at the beginning of a song, see if you can use a section from somewhere else in the song. Is the outro instrumental? Is there a bridge? Is that instrumental? Being a DJ is like being a treasure hunter at times. You are on a quest to find something within each song that you can re-use and add to your library.

HOW do I extend an intro?

Beyond creating a loop, there are other ways you can permanently create an extended intro.

There are different software programs you can use to create an edit, such as Ableton Live, Logic Pro, Pro Tools, GarageBand, Adobe Audition, Audacity, and more.

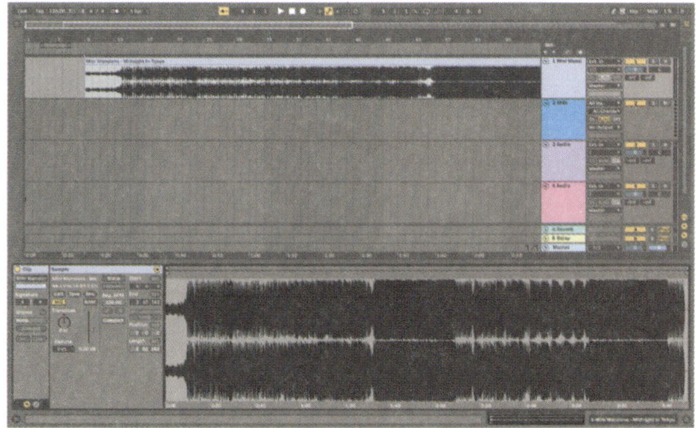

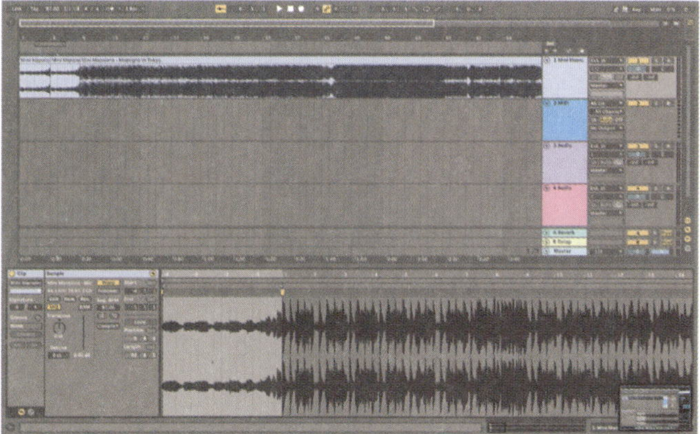

Recently, Serato launched a program called Serato Studio that was designed specifically to help DJs create their own edits, including the ability to quickly create extended intros.

For many DJs, creating edits can be a great next step in finding and developing their own unique sound. These techniques give you a better understanding of your music, and pre-producing tracks helps you blend seamlessly between songs during a performance. Creating your own edits is an intermediate-to-advanced skill, but it is becoming a necessary one for DJs to possess.

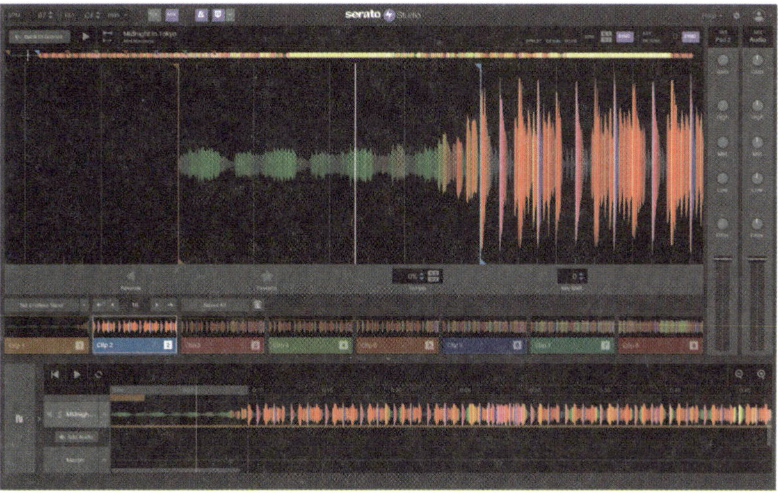

Related terms: Anatomy of the Mix, song structure, mapping, loop

CONCEPT 22:

Different Song Versions

WHAT are different song versions?

The following are different song versions: Radio, Album, Extended, Club, Quick Hit, Acapella, Instrumental, Remix, Bootleg, Mashup, and Transition.

NAME	DESCRIPTION	ALSO CALLED
Dirty	May contain questionable obscene, indecent, and profane words	Album
Clean	Eliminates most of the questionable obscene, indecent, and profane words	Radio
Superclean	Eliminates all questionable obscene, indecent, and profane words	
Acapella	Version of the song without any instrumentation. This can be a studio acapella which is the actual track with the lead vocal isolated. DIY acapellas have been made by DJs or producers by using a tool to extract the vocal frequencies from the original stereo file.	DIY Acapella
Instrumental	Version of the song without the vocals. The instrumental can be helpful for making mashups, remixes, and more.	
TV Track	Usually the TV track is designed for use by the original singer to perform with. The main lead vocal is muted, but the backing vocals are present.	
Intro	A minimum of an 8-bar instrumental intro to make mixing between songs easier	Extended, Intro - Clean, Intro - Dirty, DJ Friendly
Short	A shortened version of the song	Quick Hit, Short Edit, Jump Off
Mashup	Typically, a song that contains two distinct songs from different genres. Many times, this will be listed in the Artist field as "Artist x Artist" or the name of the song will be a creative mix of both songs, e.g., "24k Thriller."	Blend, DJ Edit
Hype	A more energetic version of the song, usually in the intro section	Build Intro, Party Break, Jump Off
Re-Drum	A song that has added drum patterns to it	
Remix	A remake of the original song. Remixes can vary greatly from something very simple like added instrumentation to a full rework.	Rework
Bootleg	A remix that is typically not an official remix from the original artist and label. Can also be a more simple remix with a new "drop" section.	Remix, Rework
Segway	A premixed transition that typically is done between two songs that share a theme, phrase, or sample	Transition
Transition	An edit that starts at one BPM tempo and finishes at another BPM tempo. This will usually be listed as BPM1 - BPM2, e.g., "125 - 70 BPM."	

WHY are different song versions important?
Music is a tool to a DJ, so these different versions are a big part of the creative process. Different versions allow more options for mixing from song to song. For example, you may have found an "acapella in" version of a song. This can be a great way to line up that acapella section underneath an instrumental section of a song you are playing. Having the acapella section will eliminate any clashing of drums and will make that mix more seamless. Another option for this type of edit would be to play the track on its own from the acapella intro as a way of changing things up. Maybe the acapella section is a well-known chorus that will have people singing along; when that section finishes, the full track will kick in and the place will erupt!

Keep in mind that you want to have access to a lot of music, but not too much. You want to make sure that you have an organized library as well, so that you can find what you are looking for. It is useless to have 100,000 songs but not know how to mix with them. In terms of the different versions, my advice is to listen to songs before you download them. Ask yourself how you would use this song. Do you need the instrumental version? Do you need all five remixes available in the digital record pool? Over time, you will discover what your sound is and what songs you would rather pass on.

WHERE do I get different song versions?
There are both digital and physical locations where you can get different song versions. Digital record pools are websites designed to be centralized distribution centers for DJs to get music. This is where a majority of professional DJs go to build their libraries. The record pools will usually have the latest releases with multiple versions for easy mixing, and instrumentals and acapellas for creative purposes.

There is no "one-stop shop" for music, and as a DJ, it's important to take pride in your collection. While you may find a majority of recent releases on a digital record pool, you will want to find other songs that may not be as popularized or available. Finding a less popular song from an album you download from Amazon or iTunes may be a great addition to your collection. Beatport is another digital music store that offers high-quality file options.

DJs can also dig into old CDs, cassette tapes, and vinyl records! There are still quite a few songs that have the "radio" or "album" version available on MP3 or through streaming services; however, the CD single or 12" vinyl single may be an elusive remix or instrumental version! You can find some gems by checking out used record stores in your neighborhood or when traveling. Some of my favorite moments as a DJ are going to a record store in a foreign country and finding something unexpected on vinyl. In every city I travel to, I make it a habit to get to a record store.

HOW do I use different song versions?
As you download music into your collection, one of the most important things to start thinking about is the difference between music you enjoy listening to and music you will use as a DJ. There is probably some overlap, but there are definitely songs in my DJ library that I wouldn't listen to on my own time. I will often look for alternate versions of songs that I gravitate toward as a listener. For instance, I play a lot of "feel good" dance music. If a new hip-hop song comes out and someone does an uptempo feel-good house version of it, I may consider adding that to my library. I may also download the original version, but now I have a different version that might blend more seamlessly into the rest of my collection.

I may download the acapella version of that song. I may even attempt to create my own remix to make it fit better into my collection. There are lots of options for utilizing alternate versions of a song. Sometimes it's even the remix that gets me interested in the original song!

Related terms: extended intros, Anatomy of the Mix, playlist, song organization

CONCEPT 23:

Pre-Cue

WHAT is pre-cue?

Pre-cue is a mode that enables you to listen to and preview the upcoming song while still playing the current one. You are doing this in your headphones, and the audience cannot hear what you're listening to.

WHY is pre-cue important?

Being able to listen to a song before it plays live is important, as it's your way to audition the transition, or get a feel for what it will sound like once the songs are together. This allows for improvisation and gives you the ability to call up a song and test it in the moment. It's risky to try a transition live, hearing it at the same time as your audience. Pre-cueing is a way to stay one step ahead of the audience and is an essential tool for any DJ.

One of the biggest joys as a DJ comes with being "present" in your performance, so that you can make adjustments in the moment based on how the crowd is responding and incorporate creative ideas on the fly. This is much more fun than playing a strictly planned-out set, and it allows you to reach a flow state.

In addition to auditioning mixes, the headphones and pre-cue are essential for manual beat-matching. If you are trying to beatmatch manually without Sync, the pre-cue allows you to hear when a song is falling off so you can cue up correctly before the audience hears it. This technique of manual beatmatching can take some time to master but is often seen as a rite of passage for a DJ.

WHERE do I pre-cue?

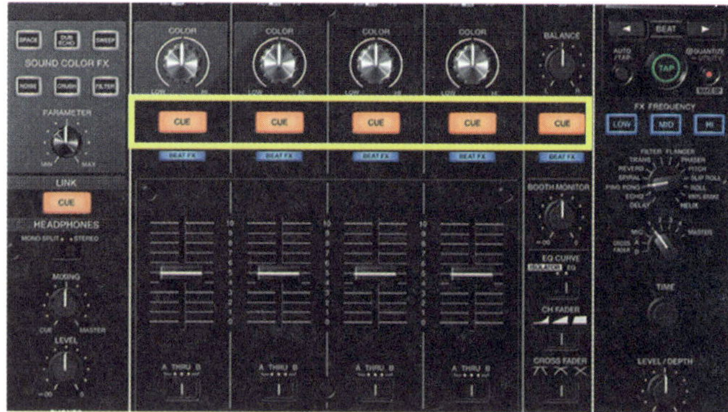

On every DJ mixer, there is an input to plug in a pair of headphones. Once you have your headphones plugged in, there is a set of standard controls you will find. There is a volume knob for the headphone volume. This volume is independent and does not affect the sound that is going out through the master speakers, so you can have the volume in your headphone set to your liking. There is also either a switch or a set of buttons that you will switch on or off to toggle between the current deck and the deck you wish to pre-cue. This is typically found either near the headphone volume if it's a switch or above the channel volume fader if it's a button. If you are playing a song on the right deck, you would turn on the pre-cue for the left deck, the one you are going to play next. You can listen to them simultaneously; however, I find that a bit confusing. I focus on listening to the song that is coming in next in my headphones, while moving my body and listening with my other ear to the music that is playing for the crowd.

There are a few more knobs and switches related to pre-cue that you may come across. One of them switches between "cue" and "master." If you flip the switch or twist the knob all the way to "master," you will hear in your headphones what is coming out of the speaker and this will disable the pre-cue. If you switch to "cue," you will hear only the pre-cue. With a knob or slider, you can find some middle ground between blending these two options, for instance 70% pre-cue, 30% master.

Another setting on some of the more expensive rigs is a switch called "split cue." Split cue will split the left and right headphone cups and will give you "cue" in your right ear and "master" in your left ear. This is a really interesting setting, and I personally love mixers with this feature. It allows me to put both headphone cups on so I can mix in situations where there is no monitoring system nearby—or if there is a delay somewhere. Split-cue is also great for practicing late at night without waking up the whole house or the neighbors.

HOW do I use pre-cue?

I used to teach my students that a DJ listens to two songs at the same time, but I've realized that this is not true. A better way to teach manual beatmatching is to focus on the song that is coming in, the song in your headphones. Your body should be moving to the song that is playing for the crowd, and you should have one headphone cup off your other ear so that you can keep track of the rhythm with that ear and your body. Then, you will be matching up what you are hearing in the headphone to what your body is moving to! (For more on manual beatmatching, see the next concept.)

As you gain experience, switching between the channels for your pre-cue will become second nature. I should also note that managing the volume of your headphones is crucial. As DJs, our hearing is something that should be protected and cherished. Try to keep the headphone volume low because once you lose a frequency, you cannot get it back! It's one of the few things that our bodies cannot repair and heal naturally.

I would also recommend finding a comfortable pair of headphones. They don't have to be the most expensive, but keep in mind that you will likely be wearing them for hours at a gig while you dance and move around behind the decks. You want to find headphones that fit well and you can keep on your head or in your ears. There are several types of headphones: *in ear*, *on ear*, and *over ear*.

ON EAR

MORE RANGE OF MOTION FOR CUPS

LIGHTER WEIGHT

CHEAPER THAN OVER EAR

OVER EAR

LESS RANGE OF MOTION FOR CUPS

HEAVIER WEIGHT

GREAT FOR STUDIO AND PERFORMANCE

IN EAR

GREAT FOR DJS WITH LONG HAIR OR HATS

MOST PORTABLE

SHORTER WIRE TO MIXER

I switched to in-ear monitors years ago and love them because they are less bulky in my bag, easy to stash in my pocket, have great sound, and work really well when I'm wearing a fedora!

IN EAR MONITORS (IEM)

CUSTOM FIT TO YOUR EARS

SUPER HIGH-QUALITY SOUND AND CUSTOMIZABLE

RELATIVELY EXPENSIVE TO PURCHASE AND REPLACE

Another tip is to avoid Bluetooth and noise-cancelling headphones. At the time of writing this, Bluetooth has not been integrated into professional DJ rigs, as there is too much latency with the signal to be effective for pre-cueing. Noise-cancelling headphones are great at home or on an airplane. However, when you are DJing, you want to be able to hear the ambient sounds, including the crowd's screaming when you nail that transition!

Related terms: headphones, cue, manual beatmatching, volume, mixing

CONCEPT 24:
Manual Beatmatching

WHAT is manual beatmatching?

Manual beatmatching is when you align the beats of two or more songs without the use of the Sync function in your software. You use the tempo fader to increase or decrease the speed of the songs and get the beats to line up. As a DJ who has been in the business for over 20 years, I started on vinyl without Sync. Most DJs who started before the digital era had to learn how to manually beatmatch, which was a big rite of passage. It can be challenging, but it's a wonderful skill to learn. It will help you better connect with the music because of the way you need to move, manipulate the track, and control the vinyl or digital platter. You can gain a lot of confidence in how you are able to take over the mix and line it back up if the beat starts to fall off.

A good analogy is driving a car with a stick shift. Today, most new drivers learn on an automatic. There's a sense of pride though that comes with driving a stick shift, or manual transmission; and even beyond that, it gives you a better understanding of how the car works and a greater sense of control.

WHY is manual beatmatching important?

Before software came along, manual beatmatching was the only way you could blend two songs together as a DJ. It's often the line in the sand that veteran DJs draw between those who *can* and those who *can't*.

Beyond earning the respect of other DJs, there's a flow state you reach when manually beatmatching. You are focused on making sure the songs stay on beat—and in order to do that, for a period of time, you are completely focused on being hands-on with the tracks and physically connected to the songs. You are forced to be in a fully present state; otherwise, you risk the beats falling off and sounding terrible to your audience. There are many things DJs do that can go unnoticed by an uninformed audience, but hearing two songs that are playing at the same time with mismatched beats is not one of those.

WHERE do I manual beatmatch?

Learning how to manual beatmatch on vinyl records is preferred but not necessary. A vinyl turntable has a large (12") surface area, which really helps with the fine adjustments, but it's also possible to emulate those same movements on smaller digital platters. Mechanically, a vinyl turntable works differently than a digital DJ controller, and this will require you to make more adjustments. The turntable itself loses its "perfect rotation" over time and needs to be tuned. This can pose an additional challenge to an amateur DJ who is learning to beatmatch. Think of this as training with ankle weights. If you can do it on a set of untuned, imperfect turntables, you can do it on a brand-new shiny DJ controller. This is one of the reasons that some veteran DJs still recommend that beginners start on vinyl turntables.

As mentioned, it's not necessary to learn on vinyl turntables, but it is important to understand that your DJ controller was designed to emulate the vinyl turntable. If you touch the top of the platter, it will stop the music, just like on a vinyl record. If you move the side of the platter in a clockwise motion, it creates a minor, temporary speed-up. If you pull back, it will temporarily slow down. This is how you would "nudge" the track forward or "pull" it back to be able to line up the beats of the song you are cueing to the song that is playing live out of the speakers.

The other setting that is essential when manual beatmatching is the Tempo slider. On a vinyl turntable, this was originally called the "pitch control." The reason for this is that by increasing the tempo, the speed of the turntable would also increase, which, in turn, would alter the pitch of the song; in other words, it would make the pitch higher. Most pitch faders maxed out at 8% slower or 8% faster on a vinyl turntable. This means that if you were to play a song that was 100 BPM, and you pitched it 8% faster, it would play at 108 BPM. If you pitched it down 8%, it would play at 92 BPM. Now, with digital DJ software, most of the Tempo sliders can be increased to 10%, 25%, 50%, or even 100% faster or slower. (For more on this, see Concept 26: Tempo Slider/Pitch Slider.)

HOW do I manual beatmatch?

Let's break this into steps. For reference, let's say Song A is 103 BPM and Song B is 104 BPM, and we are currently playing Song A out loud at its original tempo.

Step 1: Finding Songs

First of all, make sure you are finding songs that are within the same BPM range. Keep in mind that the closer they are, the easier it will be to manually beatmatch them. However, even songs that have the exact same BPM still need to be manually adjusted if you are not using Sync. In our example, we know that the songs are within range as they are just 1 BPM apart.

Step 2: Adjusting the Tempo Slider

While there's no guarantee that this will fully line up the beats, we do know that it will get us a lot closer and we can make adjustments from there. Given that Song A is playing at 103 BPM and the song we are bringing in is 104, we need to move the Tempo slider of Song B down—technically by 1% or so—to make it close to 103 BPM. If we are using DJ software, it will show a display of the track's BPM and the % of change. You could use this display, but if you really want to practice manual beatmatching and fine tune your ear, I suggest not even looking at it.

Step 3: Getting a Clean Start

As Song A continues to play, we want to make sure to start Song B on the "1" of a phrase to be certain that the beats are aligned. In order to tell which car is faster during a drag race, both cars need to have the same start. This is a similar concept. If both songs are set to the same speed, but one gets a head start, they will stay unmatched the entire time.

In order to get a clean start, your rhythm and timing have to be practiced and perfected. On a vinyl turntable, this is where a simple scratch and release comes into play, since there is a delay when hitting "play" on the vinyl turntable. With a DJ controller, the "play" button is instant and you can use this to bring in the song, or you can practice your simple scratch and release here as well.

Step 4: Making a Minor Adjustment

Assuming you get a clean start, you may find that Song B sounds like it is matched up perfectly with Song A, but over time, it starts to fall behind. At this point, you want to use your hand to speed up Song B to get it back on beat with Song A. This is definitely where the finesse comes in. You want to be able to speed it up by hand, and once you do, you want to see if that fixes the issue. If the two tracks are close enough, you can "babysit" Song B even as you mix it in live, since they will only be playing together for several bars. Again, this takes practice and finesse and is a part of the challenge!

Step 5: Making a Major Adjustment to the Tempo Fader

If you notice that after making a minor adjustment, Song B is still falling off, the issue is that it is not at 103 BPM as intended. In this case, you need to make an adjustment on the tempo fader. Using the tempo fader expands and contracts the song; so now, it's important to get back to the beginning of Song B and get another clean start to see whether that fixed the overall issue. Repeat, repeat, repeat!

Related terms: tempo, BPM, drums, headphones, pre-cue, platter adjust, music theory

CONCEPT 25:

Sync

WHAT is Sync?

Sync is the software feature that gives you the ability to match up audio files based on beat analysis. Learning how to match the beats of two different songs is fundamental to mixing as a DJ. The addition of beat Sync to DJ software has enabled DJs to worry less about matching beats and focus more on song structure, managing and manipulating sounds, and other creative aspects. Many veteran DJs claim that the Sync button is "cheating," as many of us had to go through the frustration of learning how to manually beatmatch before DJ software existed.

WHY is Sync important?

The Sync button is based on BPM and the beat grid analysis done by the software before performing. When mixing two songs together, it's important that they are beatmatched properly so that the dancefloor isn't thrown off by the jarring sound of two songs "galloping" together. Once you have your songs analyzed, you can simply hit the Sync button and it will change the BPM of the songs you are playing to be identical, essentially lining up all the beats, or beatmatching. Beatmatching is the literal matching of beats, while the term "mixing" refers to how and where you get in and out of the songs. Sync accomplishes the beatmatching aspect, but not the mixing. So, you also need to know the structure—the location and length of the song elements—in order to mix effectively.

I like to think of the Sync button as training wheels when learning to ride a bicycle. It can be a great way for an amateur DJ to get started, without having to worry about "falling off"; he or she can focus on other aspects, like song structure and fader control. This can also be a great confidence booster when first getting started.

When I started teaching others how to DJ, I wanted students to learn manual beatmatching first, but I recognized over time that it is not essential to being a good DJ. It's like telling someone they are not a good driver if they drive an automatic and do not know how to drive a stick shift. However, I do believe that if given the opportunity, DJs should learn how to manually beatmatch instead of solely relying on the technology of the Sync button.

WHERE do I find Sync?

There is a Sync button on the controller or hardware that you are using. This button corresponds with the button in the software. There may also be various Sync settings in the software's preferences. For instance, Serato DJ Pro gives you the ability to choose which type of Sync you want to use.

You can also turn Sync on and off at any time during your performance. This may be important if you are looking to change up the tempo drastically. Let's say you have been playing house music for the last hour at 120 BPM. Now, you want to switch it up and play some Latin pop music that is down at 95 BPM. At this time, you would want to disable the Sync so that you can get down to 95 BPM without the sound being distorted.

To toggle the Sync on and off, you typically just hit the Sync button again, although this may vary in some DJ software. Be sure to test how to turn the Sync on and off before playing in a live environment.

HOW do I Sync?

Similar to manual beatmatching, there are several steps you need to take in order to use Sync properly. For this example, let's say we are playing Song A at its original tempo of 103 BPM and we are getting ready to mix in Song B, which is 104 BPM.

Step 1: Make sure the song BPM and grid are correct.

Sync follows the grid. If your beat grid is incorrect (which in my experience happens about 1 in 20 times), you will need to fix the grid. Hitting Sync will sync the two songs together, but if one of the tracks is incorrect, the end result will be a complete train wreck. One way to tell is by first hitting Sync on Song B and keeping that one in your pre-cue. Do they sound good together? Are the beats off? If the beats are off, it may be that the beat grid is incorrect and you'll need to fix this. (See video and text for Concept 17: Editing Grids.)

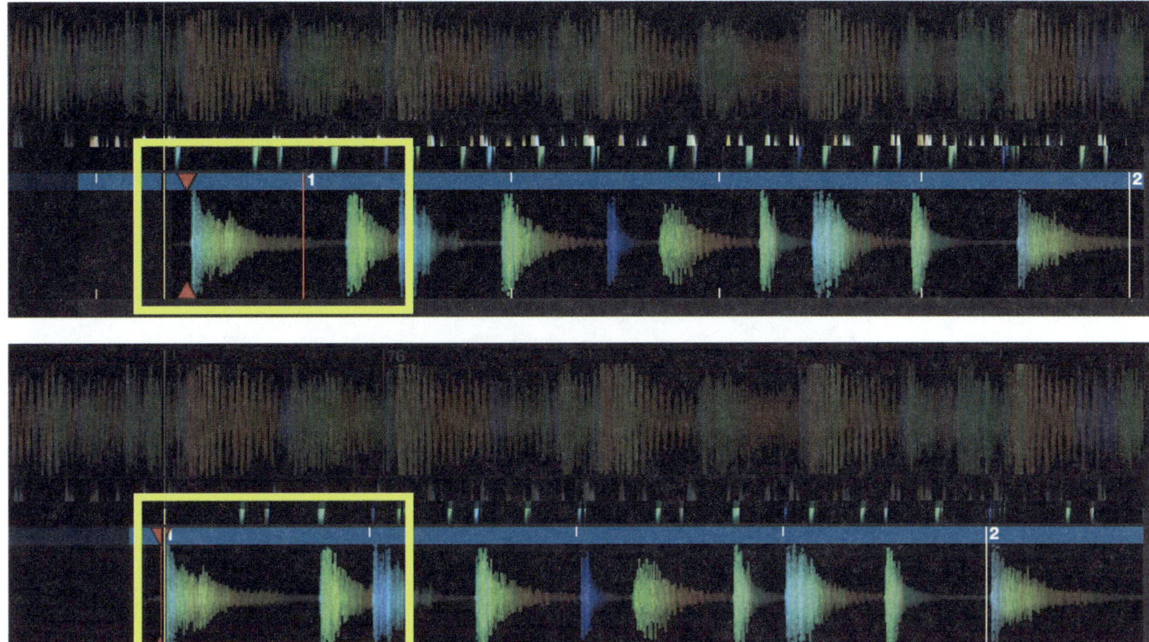

Step 2: Make sure to sync the correct deck.

Since Song A is playing, we would hit Sync on the deck that Song B is on. This is very important. We want to sync Song B to be the same tempo as Song A (103 BPM in this example), not the other way around. Once they are synchronized, we can move the Tempo slider and both tracks will change simultaneously!

Step 3: Make sure to focus on the phrasing and song structure.

By using Sync, we have eliminated quite a few steps and quite a bit of frustration. We need to make sure that the mix sounds good and that we are paying attention to how to get in and out of the songs we are mixing. We should also take this opportunity to focus on volume control and the smoothness of the mix. Another thing to consider is the vibe of the songs. Are they consistent? Will these two songs sound good together? Using Sync frees up our attention to focus on these factors.

Related terms: manual beatmatching, tempo, BPM, music theory, grid

CONCEPT 26:
Tempo Slider/Pitch Slider

WHAT is the Tempo slider?

The *Tempo slider* is a slider that changes the tempo, or BPM, of the song. Formerly the *Pitch slider* on a vinyl turntable, this slider changed the pitch/key of the song as well. When the tempo was increased, the speed of the turntable also increased, which raised the pitch of the song that was playing.

The range of the slider can vary depending on the equipment you are using, but the default tempo range used to be 8%. This means that you could increase or decrease the tempo of the song by a maximum of 8%. Now, with digital DJ software, you can change the tempo range by up to 100%, and there is also the ability to isolate the tempo and the pitch and control them independently. (For more, see Concept 27: Key/Key Lock.)

WHY is the Tempo slider important?

In many cases when beatmatching two songs, they do not have the same BPM. The Tempo slider is important for slowing down or speeding up one of the songs. You need to do this in order to match the tempo of the song you are bringing in to the one that is playing for a continuous, seamless mix. The default tempo range is usually less than 10%, but some DJ software and hardware allow you to increase up to 100%. This feature enables you to create another transition effect—you can slow the song down until it stops and use this as a way to transition into another song.

Sometimes, songs can even sound better when they are sped up or slowed down. The Tempo slider is an essential part of the DJ rig and can allow you to fully manipulate the songs you are playing.

WHERE do I find the Tempo slider?

The Tempo slider is located on the controller. There is also one typically found on the outer edge of each deck. There is a notch in the middle of the Tempo slider, which indicates the original tempo; when the slider is in this position, the song will play at its original BPM. Often, there is also a light that will indicate when you are at "0" on the Tempo slider. It's important to pay attention to which direction is faster and which is slower, as this varies depending on the DJ hardware you are using.

In the software, there's a Tempo slider in the virtual space where the decks are. You will see a "+" and "-" sign (or up and down arrows) and also what the current tempo range is set to. You can click on the tempo range to change from 8% or 10% to 25%, or even 100%, depending on the software.

HOW do I use the Tempo slider?

If you are manually beatmatching, the Tempo slider is essential for finding that magic number to create a perfect match. If you are using DJ software, the movement on the Tempo slider will correspond to the tempo range you have set. It's important to avoid moving the slider too abruptly; depending on the range you set, this can really bump it to a large degree and throw you off balance. If the tempo range is at 100% and you barely move it, it will jump up by 10% and drastically change the BPM of the song you are playing. I advise keeping the tempo range at either 6% or 8%, unless you are using the Tempo slider for an effect, as mentioned earlier.

When using Sync, most software will control both synced tracks at the same time. You do not have to move both the left- and right-deck Tempo sliders separately. This is a pretty amazing feature, as it will allow you to speed up or slow down both songs at the same time. When doing this, just keep in mind that you may need to increase the tempo range in order to make a more drastic change.

Related terms: BPM, key, manual beatmatching, Sync

CONCEPT 27:

Key/Key Lock

WHAT is key and what is Key Lock?

As with tempo, every song has an original key, often referred to as the *root key*. This is the original key that the song was written and performed in.

Each song will have a root key and depending on your level of training with music theory and harmony, you may be more familiar with Classic Key. Some will likely prefer Open Key or Camelot, which can be easier for understanding basic harmonics. (See Concept 28: Harmonic Mixing for more about Camelot keys.)

CAMELOT	CLASSIC KEY	OPEN KEY
1A	A♭m	6m
1B	B	6d
2A	E♭m	7m
2B	F♯	7d
3A	B♭m	8m
3B	D♭	8d
4A	Fm	9m
4B	A♭	9d
5A	Cm	10m
5B	E♭	10d
6A	Gm	11m
6B	B♭	11d
7A	Dm	12m
7B	F	12d
8A	Am	1m
8B	C	1d
9A	Em	2m
9B	G	2d
10A	Bm	3m
10B	D	3d
11A	F♯m	4m
11B	A	4d
12A	D♭m	5m
12B	E	5d

Key Lock fixes the pitch of a tune while letting you alter the tempo. It stops the tune from sounding lower pitched as you slow it down and higher pitched as you speed it up. Key Lock maintains the original key.

WHY is Key Lock important?

When you are mixing melodic sections, it is important to maintain the key. Keeping the original key helps maintain the essence of the song. With the Key Lock on, even if you change the tempo of the song, the audience will not detect it because the vocals and melodic elements are not being *transposed*; in other words, the key is not being changed. I highly recommend trying this on your DJ rig. Move the Tempo slider up to +6% or so and listen to the song without Key Lock on. Then, turn it on and notice the difference!

WHERE do I find Key Lock?
You will find Key Lock on the virtual deck in your DJ software. It can be represented as a music note or sometimes will conveniently just say "Key Lock." Inside the browser section of your DJ software, you can select which columns you want to see, for example: Song Title, Artist, BPM, etc. Key is usually not a default field, so you may need to enable it. To do that, you can go to the top browser bar where the other categories are and right-click or control-click and select the fields you wish to show. From there, you can click on the Key column, which enables you to sort by key.

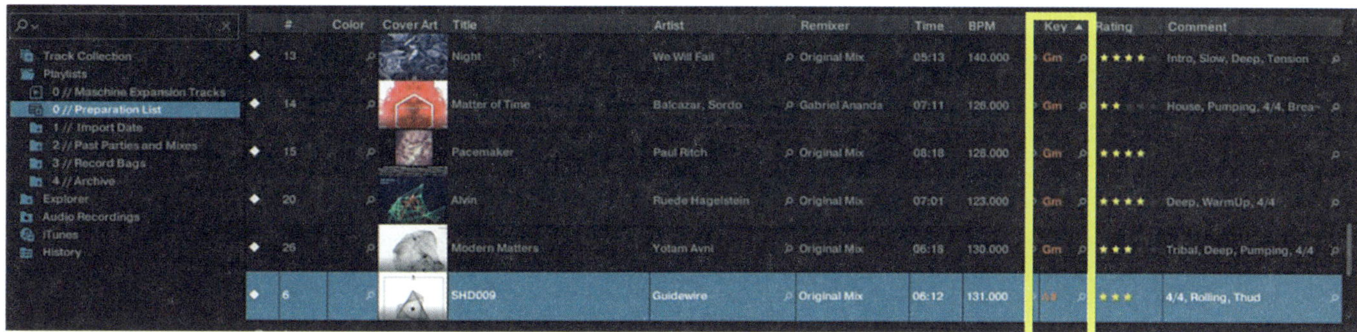

Also, when loading a song onto a deck, there will often be a place for the key to be displayed as well.

HOW do I use Key Lock?
You should turn the Key Lock on when mixing and changing the tempo. I like to keep it on throughout my set. It allows me to play a Michael Jackson song and speed it up by 3% without MJ's vocals getting too pitchy and people giving me a weird look as if I were butchering the song. In fact, most DJs are playing your favorite songs at a tempo other than the original tempo, but it's hard to notice thanks to Key Lock. Most DJ software will remember this setting and keep it on even when you log out and log back on later.

There are some software settings and features that are not mapped to buttons on the DJ controller. Key Lock is one of those features. While there is a way to toggle this inside the software, most DJ controllers do not have a dedicated button to quickly enable or disable it on the physical controller.

In some cases, Key Lock is labeled as "Master Tempo."

Related terms: harmonic mixing, tempo, tempo fader, BPM

CONCEPT 28:
Harmonic Mixing

WHAT is harmonic mixing?

Harmonic mixing, or *key mixing*, is a DJ's continuous mix between songs that are either in the same key or in different keys that are complementary to one another.

WHY is harmonic mixing important?

Let's say you are trying to mix two songs together. One of the songs has harmonic elements such as a guitar riff and synth, and the other song has drums and guitar. If these elements are not harmonically "in key," they will produce a key clash. Imagine you are listening to a band and the bassist is playing in a completely different key than the lead guitar. This would not sound good. DJs do not have access to some of these particular stems of a song. Instead, we have a completed track that we are trying to mix on top of another completed track. You could fix the problem in the example above by telling the guitar player to listen in and change the key he or she is playing in. We don't have that same luxury as DJs mixing these songs.

While understanding key and finding complementary songs is important, keep in mind that it is not essential for every mix. With most transitions, there is a fairly short amount of time that these two songs are playing together. Also, depending on the sections of the songs you are using, you may be able to play two songs that have conflicting keys by only layering portions that don't have harmonic elements. For example, the chorus in Song A may have guitar and piano, while the intro for Song B has only drums. Because you're not mixing two harmonic elements together, the keys of those songs may not matter as much and the transition could still work out well.

WHERE do I use harmonic mixing?

Most DJ software will analyze your files and try to determine the key of the song. This is similar to the beat analysis that is done to determine the tempo and set the grid—and much like beat analysis, the key analysis may not be 100% accurate. It's important to trust your ear and be willing to experiment to see how the songs sound together. I have done plenty of mixes that, technically, should not have worked according to the software's key analysis, but they sounded great anyway! Harmonic mixing is most important when mixing two harmonic sections together, creating a mashup or live remix, or adding a harmonic loop on top of a track (adding a guitar riff on top of a synth drop, for instance).

Some programs allow you to change the key of a song. In some cases, you can even use *Key Sync*, which automatically changes the song you are bringing in to a key that is complementary to the song that is playing. This works in a similar way to beat sync.

In the DJ software, you are able to change the key in increments of semi-tones (or half steps). Twelve semi-tones allow you to go one full octave higher or lower. This control is typically found on the track's virtual deck; however, some DJ hardware offers this control with physical buttons.

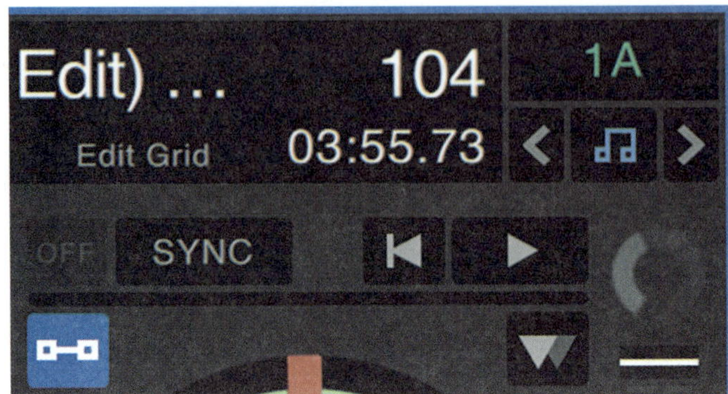

HOW do I use harmonic mixing?

If you are like me and are not a classically trained musician, you can use the Camelot system that was developed by the team at Mixed In Key. They have taken the concept of the "circle of 5ths" and assigned each key an alphanumeric value. This system makes it much easier to understand mixing in key.

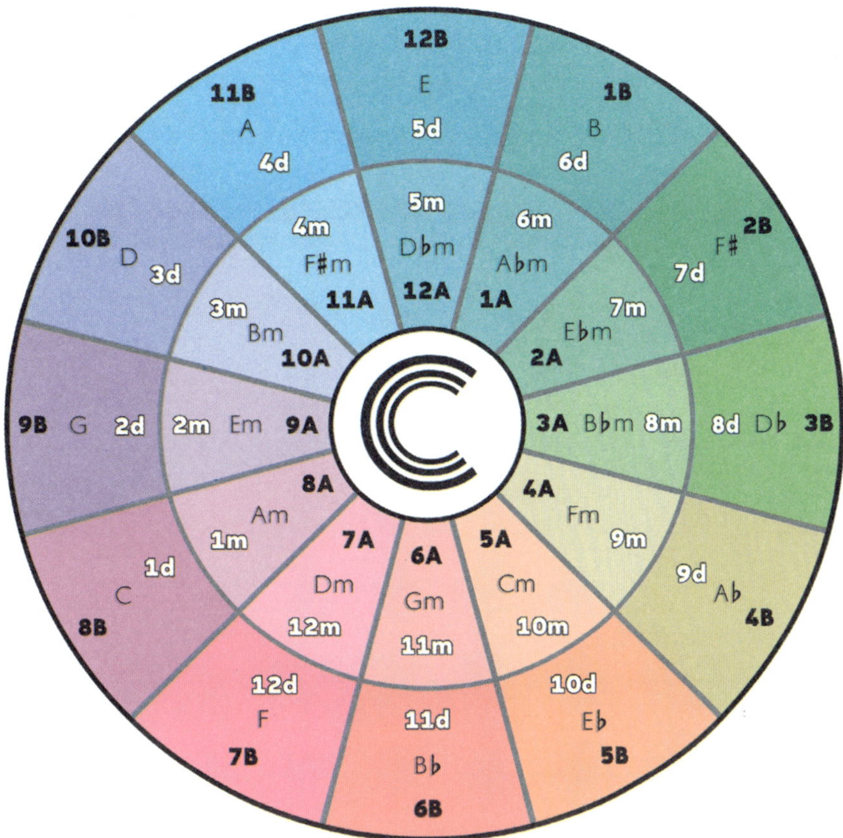

If a song is 2A on the Camelot Wheel, it can be mixed with 2B, 1A, or 3A, depicting one step to the left or right. Many DJs and music producers have that wheel on their desktop for reference.

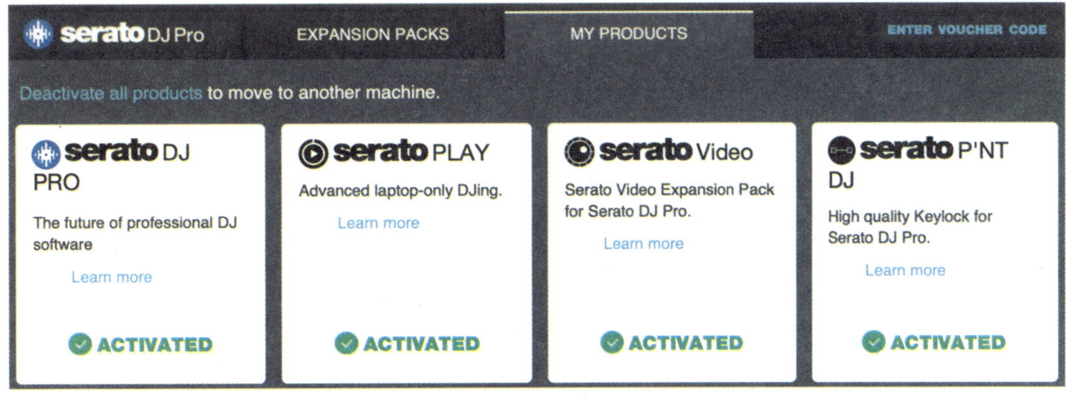

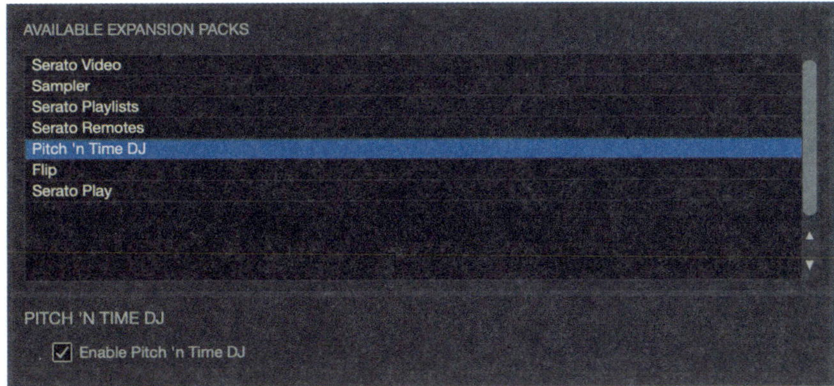

Expansion packs are often available with DJ software, including special Key Lock features.

Related terms: key, Key Lock, mixing, mashups, music theory

CONCEPT 29:
Non-Rhythm FX

WHAT are non-rhythm FX?

FX stands for "effects" and can be found as an abbreviation in your DJ software or hardware. Audio effects are analog or digital devices used to intentionally alter how a musical instrument or other audio source sounds. Effects can be subtle or extreme, and they can be used in live or recording situations.

RHYTHM FX	NON-RHYTHM FX
Delay	Reverb
Echo	Pan
Spiral	Filter
Reverse Delay	Flanger
MT Delay	Phaser
Up Echo	Robot
Down Echo	Pitch
Trans	Enigma Jet
Gate	Mobius Saw
Roll	Mobius Tri
Slip Roll	LFO Filter
Reverse Roll	Distortion
Low Cut Echo	LPF
Echo Out	HPF

Non-rhythm FX are not based on rhythm or timing when launched. Some examples include: Filter, Phaser, Flanger, Jet, High Pass Filter (HPF), Low Pass Filter (LPF), and Noise. Keep in mind that you can set parameters on each of these to change or morph depending on the beat, but in themselves they are not dependent on the rhythm and timing.

WHY are non-rhythm FX important?

Non-rhythm FX are important because they can add a dynamic element to a track. You can bend frequencies and add dynamics to a track to catch the ear of your audience. Particularly in electronic dance music, there is a constant building and releasing of tension, and many of these non-rhythm FX help to enhance that tension. For instance, using a High Pass Filter during a buildup will create more anticipation. When the build is over and the drop hits, it's important to release that Filter simultaneously so that it enhances the emphasis of the drop section.

Non-rhythm FX can also help create smoother transitions when mixing between songs. A Low Pass Filter might be very effective when trying to mix two songs together, as it will eliminate some of the high and mid frequencies of the current song and allow the new song to take on that frequency space.

WHERE do I find non-rhythm FX?

Filter is one of the most popular non-rhythm FX and has its own special place on most mixers. It has a position usually beneath the EQ (see Concept 4: EQ). Other non-rhythm FX can be found in the DJ hardware or software. Some mixers have audio effects built into them already, so you don't need software to use them. It may be tough initially to figure out which effects are rhythm based and which are not. With all audio effects, it's a good idea to try them out first and see which ones you like and which ones you don't.

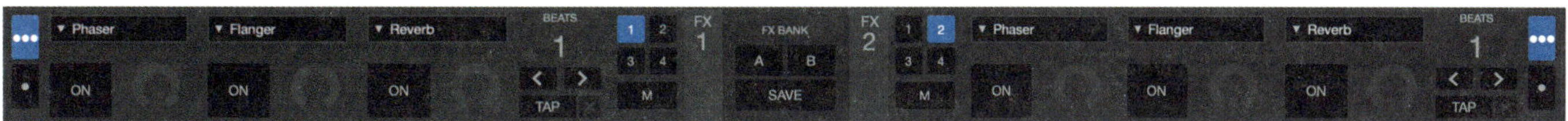

In your DJ software, you can find a tab specifically designed for the FX. You may be able to layer multiple effects together, and you will probably see a set of parameters to control each individual effect. There are typically some default effects, and most programs allow you to dig through a drop-down list of even more options for additional effects.

HOW do I use non-rhythm FX?

First, you need to choose the effect. With non-rhythm FX, it's important to identify which effect will sound good based on the type of song you are playing and when you want to use that effect. Also, you need to consider the type of sound you want to create. If you are looking for a sweeping, breathy sound, you may want to use Noise or Whitenoise. If you are looking for something futuristic and synthy sounding, you may want to use Phaser or Flanger.

Step 1: Find the effect you want.

Step 2: Assign it to the proper channel.

Next, you want to make sure it is assigned to the channel, or side, that you want it on. Also, make sure it is not set to both channels because that will affect the entire mix.

Step 3: How much saturation?

Next, you have to determine the amount of FX, or *saturation*, you want. Do you want a subtle Flanger effect or do you want to fully saturate the mix as it's playing? Saturation controls the amount of the effect and is also known as the "dry/wet knob." When the effect is completely "dry," it means 0% of the effect is being applied. If the effect is completely "wet," then 100% of the effect is being applied.

Step 4: Less is more!

Keep in mind that you don't want to overdo the audio effects. Think of FX like seasoning when cooking. Just the right amount of salt can make the dish come to life, and too much of it can ruin the dish.

Related terms: rhythm FX, Echo, dry/wet

CONCEPT 30:
Rhythm FX

WHAT are rhythm FX?

Rhythm FX are audio effects that are primarily based on rhythm. They should be set to the song's tempo. There is a smaller margin of error with these types of audio effects. When not set on time properly, they can produce jarring sounds that can throw off an entire mix. When applying rhythm FX—such as Echo, Dub Echo, Delay, Roll, or Gate—you want to make sure the BPM and grid are correct.

RHYTHM FX	NON-RHYTHM FX
Delay	Reverb
Echo	Pan
Spiral	Filter
Reverse Delay	Flanger
MT Delay	Phaser
Up Echo	Robot
Down Echo	Pitch
Trans	Enigma Jet
Gate	Mobius Saw
Roll	Mobius Tri
Slip Roll	LFO Filter
Reverse Roll	Distortion
Low Cut Echo	LPF
Echo Out	HPF

WHY are rhythm FX important?

Using FX like Echo, and other combinations of Echo effects, can be a great way to switch up the tempo, vibe, or energy in a performance. Like the non-rhythm effects, any of these can add texture to a song and create more dynamics to the overall mix. For instance, adding a 1/2-beat delay can create a sense of added percussion or reinforcement.

When transitioning between songs, an Echo or Roll effect—in combination with the EQ (see Concept 4: EQ) or volume—can create a repeating element that makes the transition from one song to another smoother.

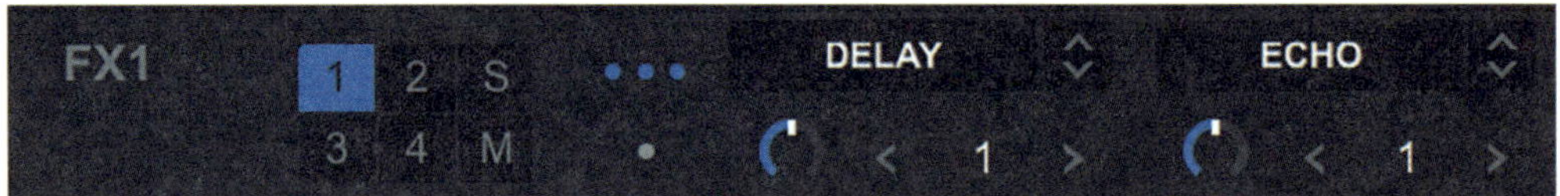

WHERE do I find rhythm FX?

Rhythm FX can be found in DJ hardware or software. Some DJ mixers have audio effects built into them already and you don't need software to use them. It may be tough initially to figure out which effects are rhythm based and which are not. With all audio effects, it's a good idea to try them out first and see which ones you like and which ones you don't.

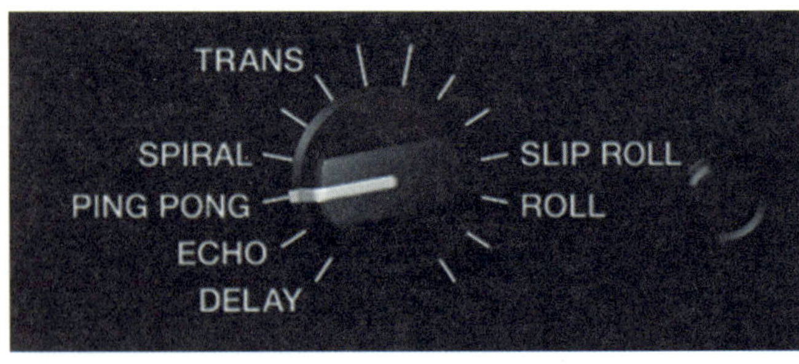

In your DJ software, you can find a tab specifically designed for the FX. You may be able to layer multiple effects together, and you will probably see a set of parameters to control each individual effect. There are typically some default effects, and most programs allow you to dig through a drop-down list of even more options for additional effects.

HOW do I use rhythm FX?

First, you need to choose the effect. With rhythm effects, it's important to identify which effect will sound good based on the type of song you are playing and when you want to use that effect. The other thing to consider is the type of sound you are looking to create. If you want to create a sound that repeats, consider an Echo or Delay. If you are looking for something that will help cut out sound rhythmically, a Gate will do.

Step 1: Select your FX.

Step 2: Assign the channel.

Next, you want to make sure it is assigned to the channel, or side, you want it on. Also, make sure it is not set to both channels because it will affect the entire mix.

Step 3: Make sure the BPM is correct.

The rhythm effect is going to follow this tempo. In other words, if you want to set a 1-beat Echo and the BPM is set to 108, the result will be a 1-beat Echo at 108 BPM. If the song is actually 95 BPM, this will sound horrible.

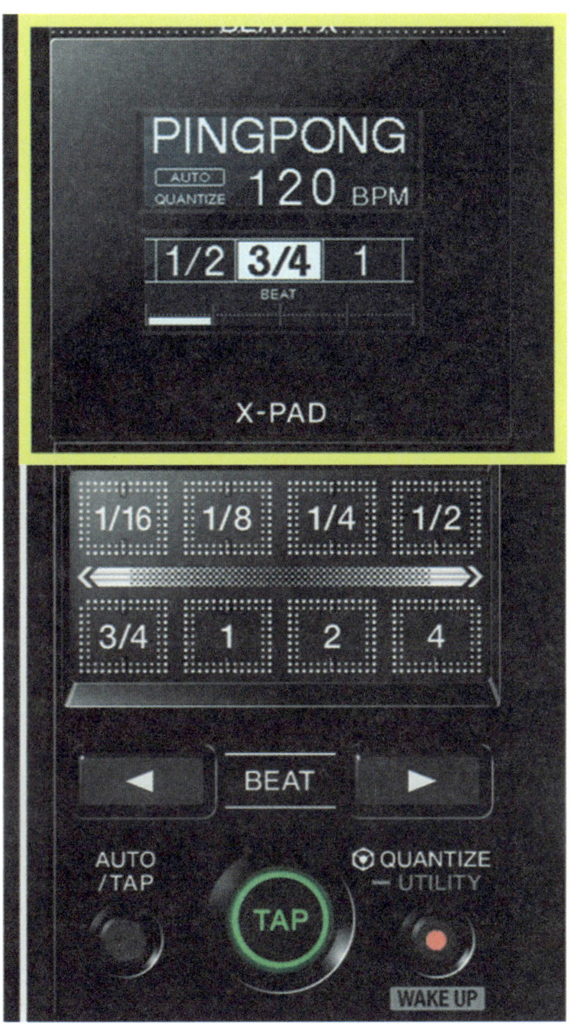

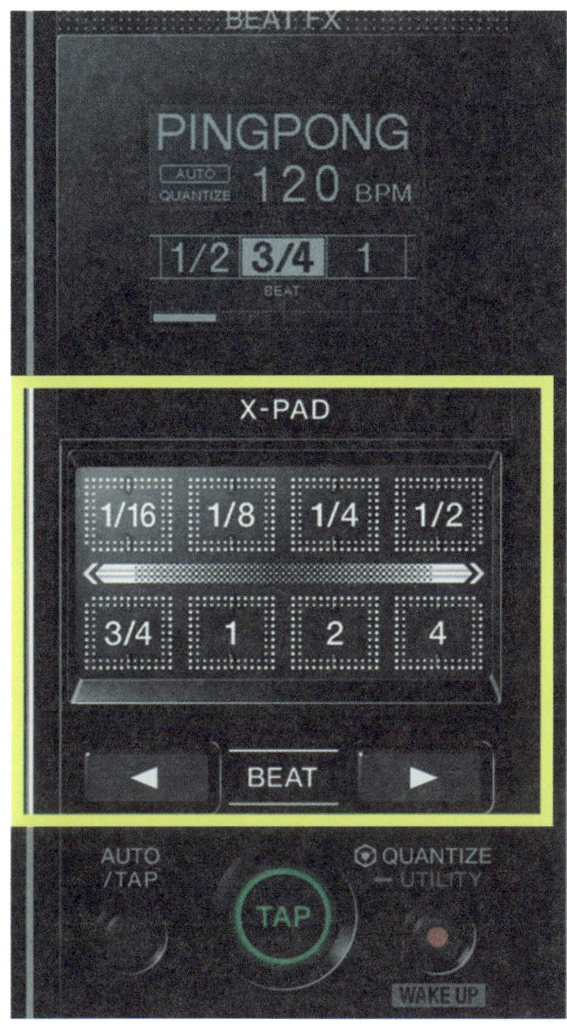

Step 4: Set the parameter timing.

The next thing you need to do is set the parameter timing. This is based on the tempo of the song that is playing. Do you want a 1-beat Echo? A 1/2-beat Echo? Some mixers actually have quick keys that set the direct timing for the effects.

Step 5: How much saturation?

Determine the amount, or saturation, of FX you want. Do you want a subtle Delay or full saturation in the mix as it's playing? Saturation controls the amount of the effect and is also known as the "dry/wet knob." When the effect is completely "dry," it means 0% of the effect is being applied. If the effect is completely "wet," then 100% of the effect is being applied.

Step 6: Less is more!

Keep in mind that you don't want to overdo the audio effects. Think of FX like seasoning when cooking. Just the right amount of salt can make the dish come to life, and too much of it can ruin the dish.

Related terms: non-rhythm FX, Echo, dry/wet

CONCEPT 31:

Changing Tempo

WHAT is changing the tempo?

Changing the tempo refers to deliberately changing from one tempo range to another, where the two BPMs are significantly different. This act of switching the tempo in a somewhat abrupt way requires practice, but it can be a great way to switch up the vibe.

WHY is changing the tempo important?

One of the fundamental skills that DJs learn is how to seamlessly blend from song to song, with a portion of the songs being played simultaneously. However, what if you don't want to stay at the same tempo all night? What if you have a request that you want to satisfy?

Learning how to control the music and change things up is important, but it can be nerve-wracking for amateur DJs. There are some songs that have even more impact coming in after silence, or "dropped on the 1," instead of being mixed in.

Just as learning to blend songs together is a fundamental skill, so is being able to effectively drop on the 1 and change up the tempo.

WHERE should I change tempo?

The key to executing a good tempo change comes down to understanding the music. It's still important to respect the song that is playing and to find a natural place to get out of that song. A great option for this is after the chorus or other high point of the song. Another option might be a low part of the song, such as a breakdown, or a section that has less instrumentation.

Equally important, you want to make sure to find a song that has what I like to refer to as a "cold start." When blending songs together seamlessly, we tend to be on the hunt for the extended intro versions, but when changing up tempo, we are looking for songs that start immediately. Preferably, the start is recognizable or catchy and can generate a big crowd reaction. A great example of this is the intro of "Humble" by Kendrick Lamar. The song even starts with a vinyl scratch sound without any beat behind it. This can be a great way to transition to a new tempo, in this case 75 BPM, at which point we can start mixing songs together that are within that range.

HOW do I change tempo?

Here are some steps to keep in mind when changing up tempo:

Step 1: Make sure to identify the song you are going into.

Find a song with a recognizable intro. Sometimes, you may need to find a song to help you get to the tempo that you want, so you can get to other songs you want to play. There are some songs that can be seen as a "means to an end."

75	4A	***Humble. (Clean)	Kendrick Lamar	COLD START!
75	4A	***Humble. (Dirty)	Kendrick Lamar	COLD START!
75	4A	Humble. (Intro Clean)	Kendrick Lamar	

Step 2: Use a simple echo effect or fade out.

Be sure to respect the structure of the song you are coming out of, and then set a loop or use a simple Echo Out effect to create some space. This will alert your dancefloor that something is about to happen and they will likely stop moving. Don't be afraid of this moment. You just need to have the new song ready to go and have some confidence for the next step.

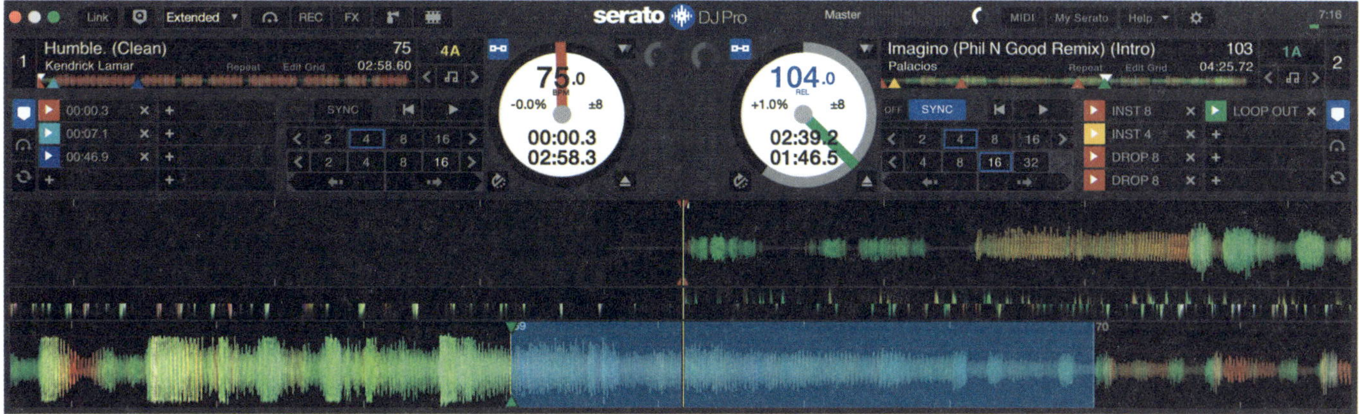

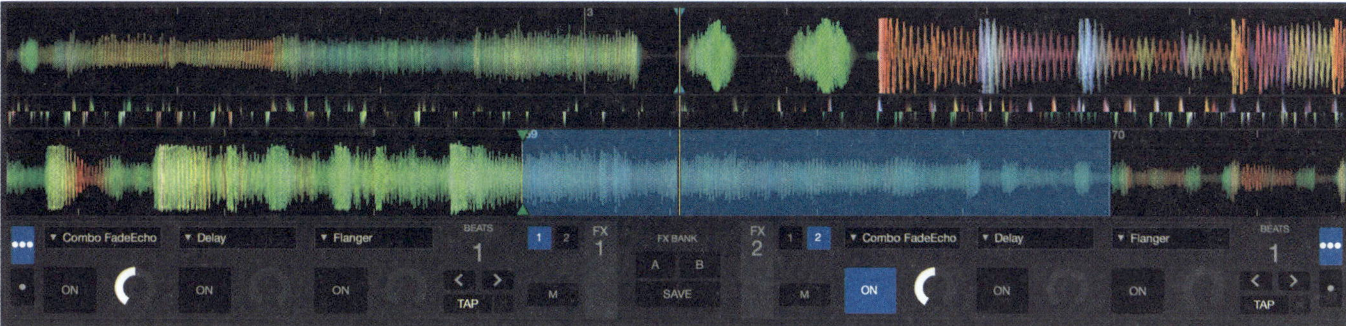

Step 3: Bring in the new song with confidence.

They will stop and look in your direction and you need to be ready. You can simply hit play on the song, or even better, give it a quick scratch and release it. If you have made a good song choice, it may be one of the biggest reactions of the set.

Also, keep in mind that if you typically mix with Sync on, you want to make sure to turn that off. Some DJs also like to add a sound effect, such as a siren or airhorn to add more energy to the transition.

Related terms: rhythm FX, BPM, song structure, Anatomy of the Mix

CONCEPT 32:

Smoothing Out the Mix

WHAT is smoothing out the mix?

The Filter effect and the equalizer can be great ways to eliminate some of the extra frequencies you have when mixing and blending two songs together. Remember, EQ is typically divided into three knobs on a DJ controller: High, Mid, and Low. These knobs represent their respective frequencies (see Concept 4: EQ). Most DJ controllers also have a dedicated Filter knob on each channel, which allows for easy access when controlling a mix.

WHY is smoothing out the mix important?

After understanding the Anatomy of the Mix and how to map out songs (see Concept 3: Mapping Out Songs), the next step is to find better ways to smooth out the mix. When you have two songs playing simultaneously and at the same volume, every frequency is doubled. By using a combination of the EQ and Filter, you can better blend the two songs together. For instance, if Song A and Song B are playing at the same time, I may want to reduce the low frequency on Song A as I bring in Song B. That way, the listeners can get acclimated to the new bottom end of Song B, while still hearing the mid and high frequencies of Song A.

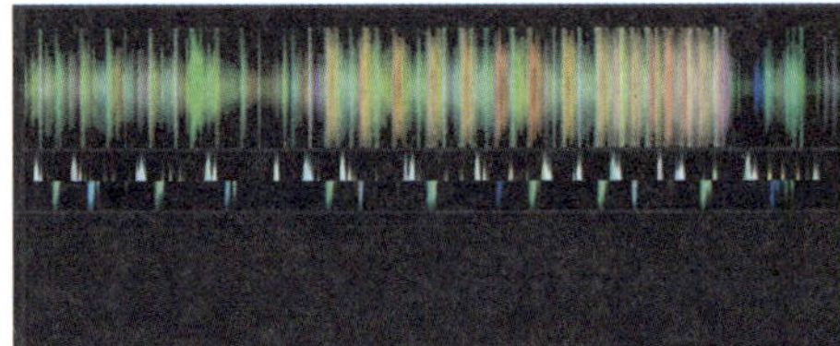 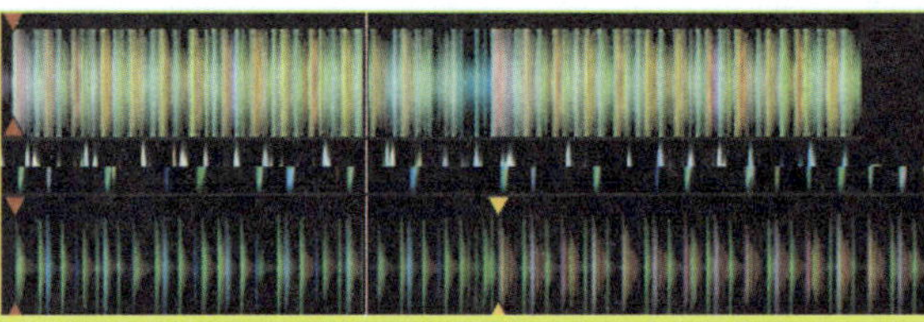 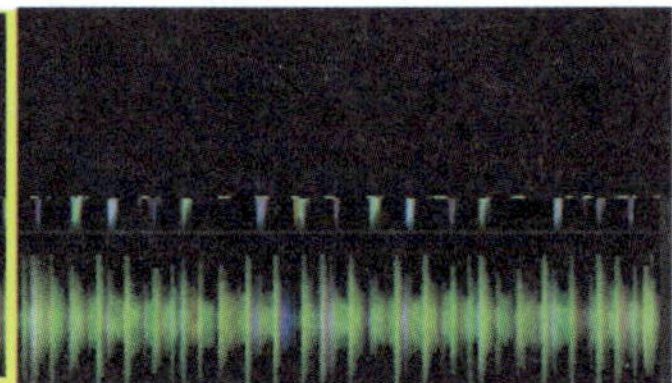

WHERE do I start to smooth out the mix?

The EQ and Filter knobs are usually found in the center of the mixer or controller. They are in a vertical row, usually starting with the High knob at the top, followed by the Mid, Low, and then Filter. There should be a notch in the middle of each knob when the line on the knob is aligned vertically at 12 o'clock.

As you begin to blend two songs together, you can start with the EQ knobs down, but this will affect what you are hearing in your pre-cue. Instead, I pre-cue with the EQ fully up—but as I begin to mix, I start to bring the frequencies down and up accordingly. This process is about experimenting and being in the present moment. Each mix will sound slightly different and, depending on the songs you are mixing together, may require more or less of the different frequencies. No matter where you start mixing, you want to make sure you have reset the EQ knobs and the Filter of the new song as you stop the song you were coming out of.

HOW do I smooth out the mix?

Following are some steps showing how you could use the EQ or Filter in a mix. In this example, let's assume we are mixing Song A and Song B for a total of 16 bars.

Step 1: Be sure to follow the map you have set.

Understanding the song structure is the most important part of creating a smooth mix. As the mixpoint comes around, we are making sure that we are getting a clean start so that the two songs are beatmatched properly.

Step 2: Start to bring up the volume of Song B.

As Song A is playing, start to bring in the volume of Song B. This should be done smoothly and over the course of the first 4 bars or so.

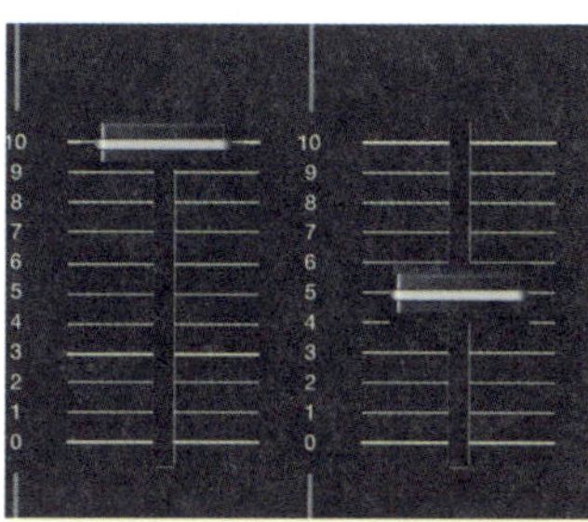

Step 3: Take out the low end of Song B as the volume comes up.

This will ensure that the low frequencies are not doubled up. You can keep the Mid and High at 12 o'clock or choose to take those down a little as well.

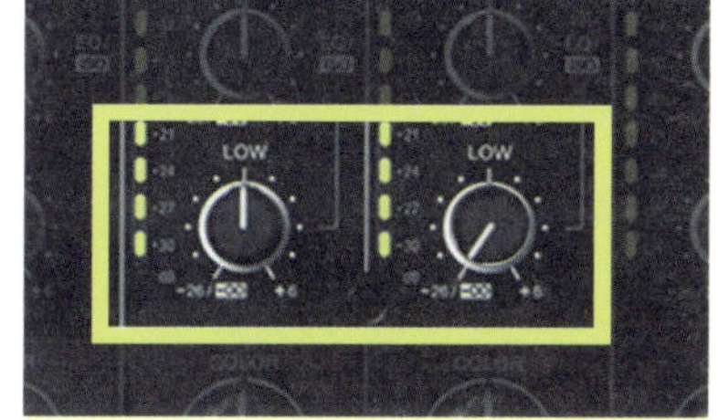

Step 4: With about 8 bars left in the mix, start to swap out the low end between songs.

As you are bringing in the low end of Song B, start bringing the low-end frequencies out of Song A. This is sometimes referred to as a *bass swap*.

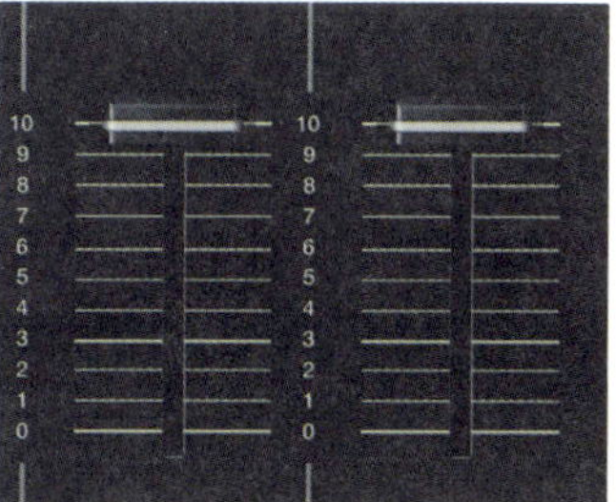

Step 5: Complete the mix by lowering the volume of Song A.

Smoothly drop the volume out of Song A at the end of the 16th bar to finish the mix.

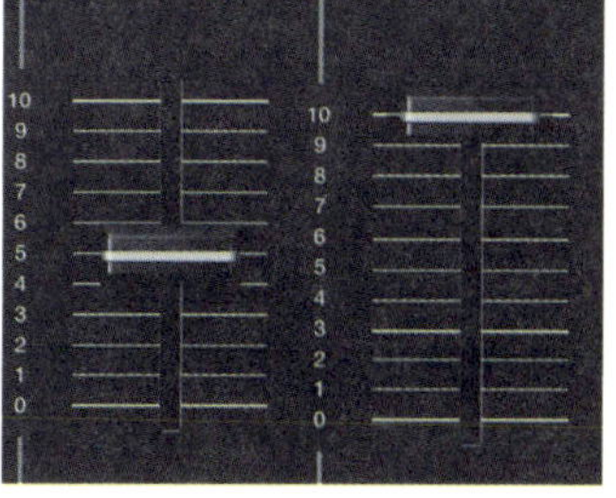

Related terms: non-rhythm FX, Anatomy of the Mix, HPF, LPF, EQ

CONCEPT 33:

Prepare Mode

WHAT is Prepare mode?

Prepare mode allows you to identify songs you want to play at some point without loading them onto the deck or having to put them into a separate playlist or crate. Prepare mode is a temporary folder. The songs in this folder will typically be deleted once they have been played live on one of the decks. The Prepare List can sometimes be referred to as a "Tag List" (rekordbox).

Tag List in rekordbox software

WHY is Prepare mode important?

There are two great reasons to use the Prepare mode:

Reason 1: Requests or a List of Songs that You Know You Want to Play at Some Point

As you are going through your library while performing, you may notice a song that you want to play, but it won't work at that moment. Loading this song into the Prepare window can be a great way to make a note of that song without derailing you from the current vibe. It will also ensure that you won't forget the song as you continue to go about your set.

Reason 2: Preparing Your Set

When going through your music before a gig, you can quickly load songs into the Prepare window without having to drag each one into a particular playlist. Once you have compiled a good number of songs, you can "select all" (Ctrl + A or Command-A) and then drag them as a batch to the playlist you want.

WHERE do I find the Prepare mode?

The Prepare window may be hidden initially. Since it's not a window that always needs to be open, you will probably have to look for it in your software and click on it to open the folder. Remember, you can close this window without losing that list; however, when you log out of your software, the Prepare List will be reset.

HOW do I use Prepare mode?

Learning keyboard shortcuts can be really useful, especially when you want to search through your library and quickly tag or prepare songs. In Serato DJ software, the shortcut Command-P quickly puts the song in the Prepare window. In other DJ software, you have the ability to create a shortcut by teaching the software what key commands you want to use. Creating a shortcut for "Add to Tag List" or "Add to Prepare" is a very helpful tool. (See Concept 39: Keyboard Shortcuts.)

Here are some steps for using Prepare mode to speed up your workflow when prepping for a gig:

Step 1: Open up the Prepare mode window.

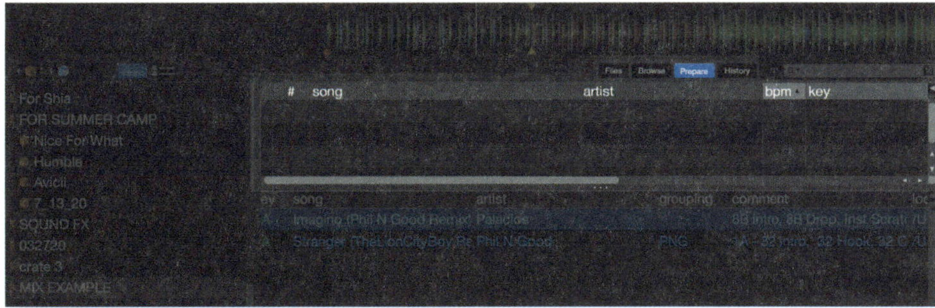

Step 2: Search through your crates or your full collection.

When you find a song you think you want to play, hit Command-P. This will add the file to the Prepare window.

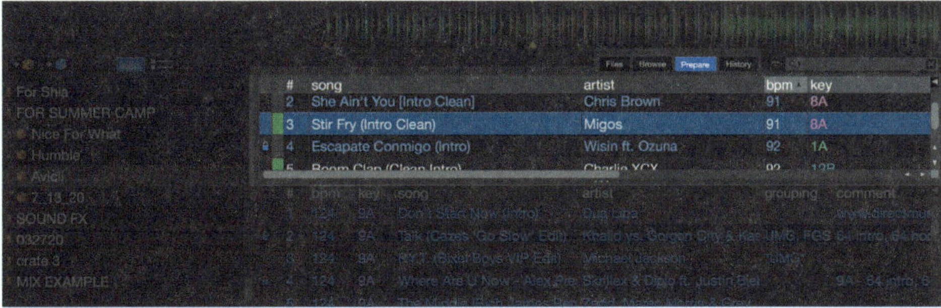

Step 3: When you have gathered up a good number of songs, use shortcut Command-A to Select All.

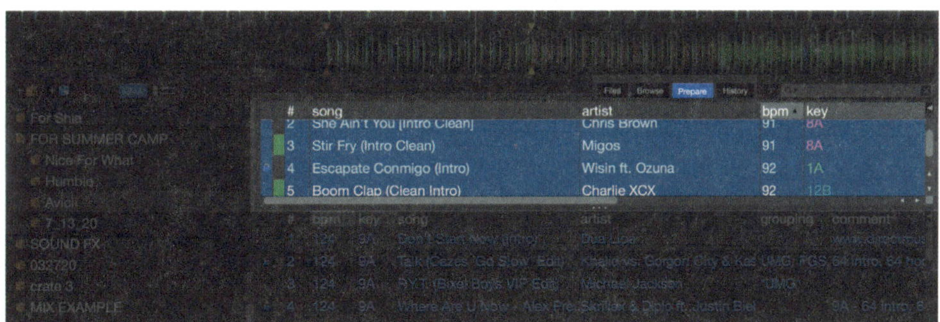

Step 4: Drag the songs into the crate area.

This will create a new crate around the songs you have selected in the Prepare mode.

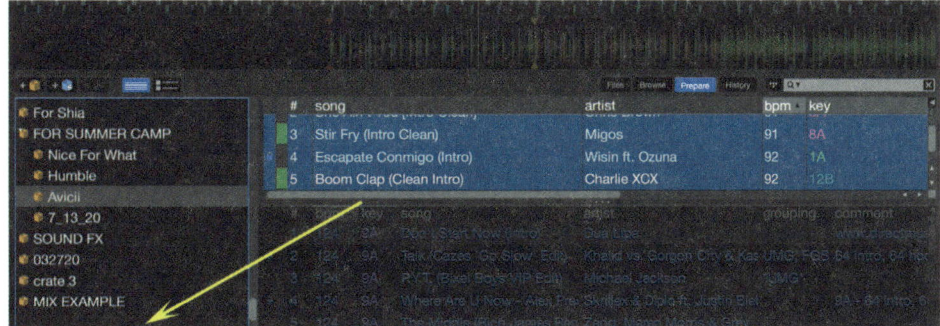

This will certainly cut down on the time and frustration of dragging each individual song into a crate. Instead, you can do it in batches!

Related terms: non-rhythm FX, Anatomy of the Mix, Filter, EQ

CONCEPT 34:

Loop Roll

WHAT is Loop Roll?

Loop Roll performs a standard Auto Loop. However, when the loop is turned off, playback returns to the position where it would be if it had not entered the loop. Loop Roll lengths are determined by the range selected in the Auto Loop tab and usually range from 1/32 to 32 beats.

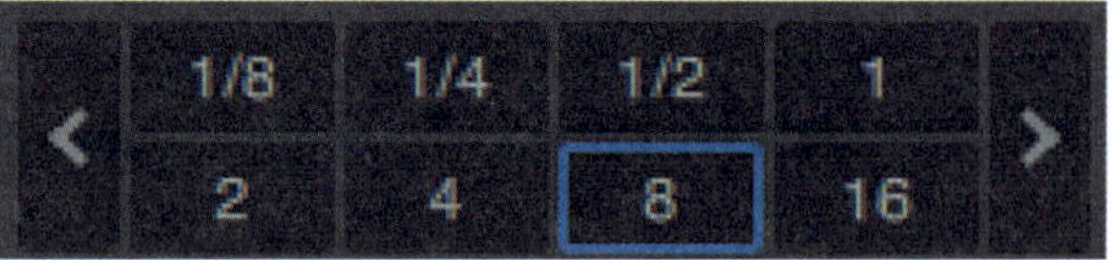

WHY is the Loop Roll important?

The Loop Roll can be a great way to quickly grab a loop, especially for a particular phrase or word. This can expand your creativity during performance. The Loop Roll is not as disruptive as setting and releasing a standard loop, since the track keeps going underneath. When you release the Loop Roll, the song picks up right where it would have been if you hadn't set it.

A Loop Roll can also be used to create and release tension. This can be particularly helpful for creating or enhancing a build section before a chorus or drop.

WHERE do I find the Loop Roll?

On most DJ controllers, there is a subpanel titled "Roll." This will convert the performance pads to now create Loop Rolls based on their assigned lengths.

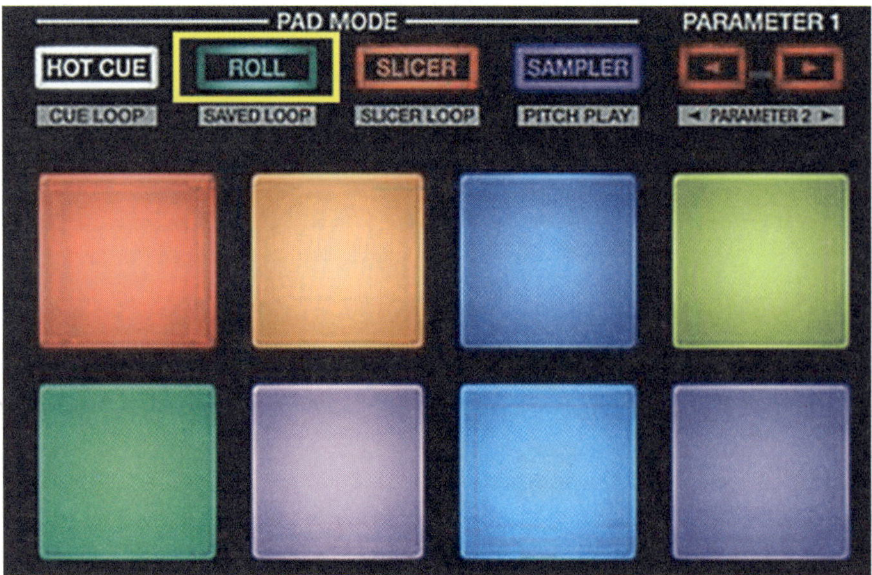

HOW do I use Loop Roll?

Here's how you could use Loop Roll to enhance a build before a drop section:

Step 1: Understand the song structure and length of the build section before the drop.

In this scenario, let's assume this section is 8 bars long.

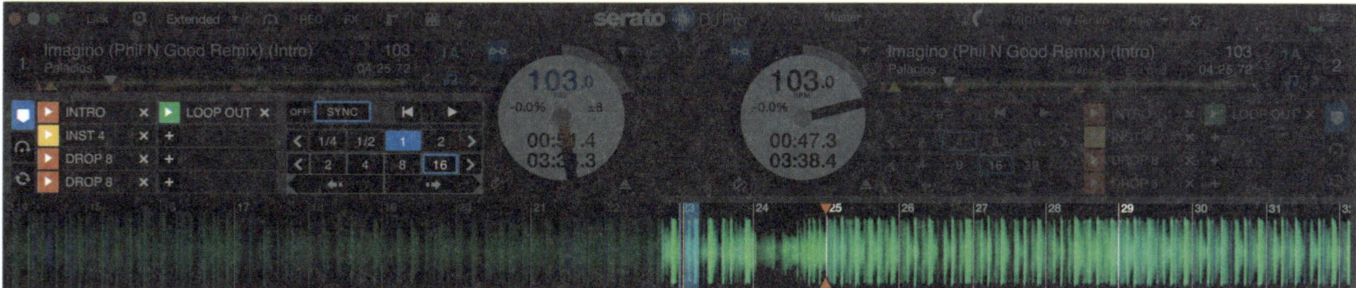

Step 2: Check to see which performance pads represent which lengths.

You may need to extend the parameter by using the parameter buttons near the loop lengths.

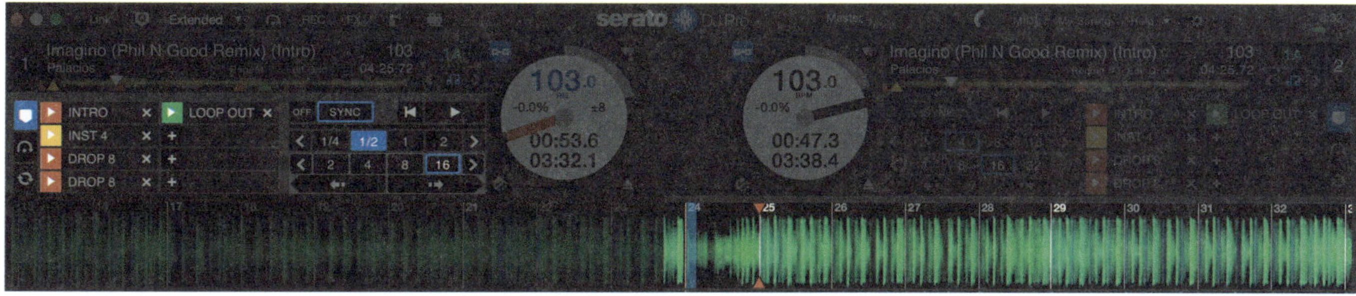

Step 3: Start with a 1-beat loop and begin to reduce its length.

Hold the 1-beat loop on the 6th bar and hold it for a bar, then jump to the 1/2-beat loop button and hold that for a bar. Then jump to the 1/4-beat loop button and hold that for half a bar. Then go to the 1/8-beat button for half a bar.

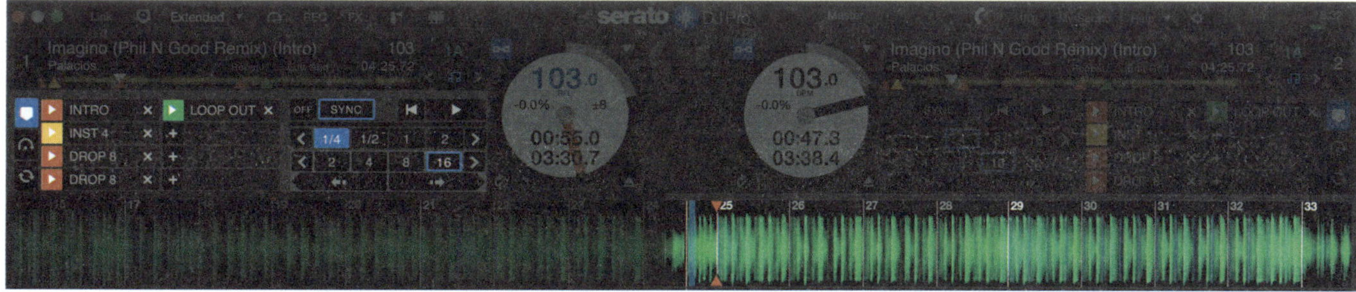

Step 4: Release the Loop Roll right before the drop.

To create even more tension, you can use the Filter knob in combination with the Loop Roll to produce a sweeping effect as the loop length gets shorter (see Concept 32: Smoothing Out the Mix).

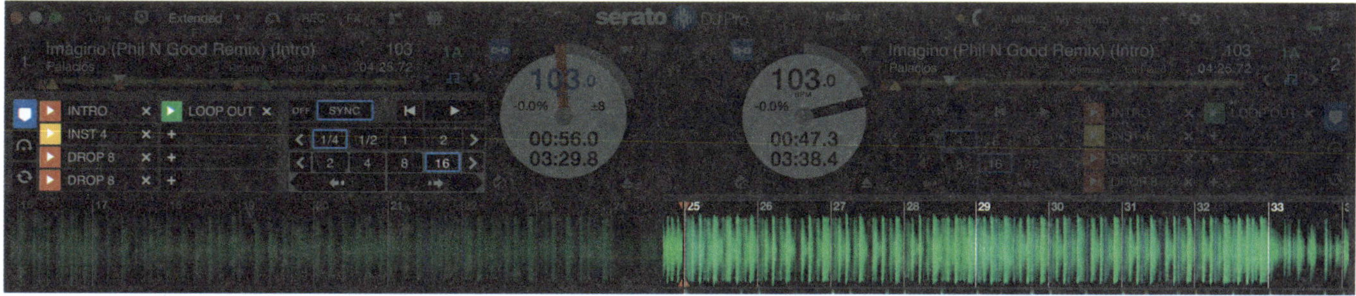

Related terms: loop, music theory, notes, note structure

CONCEPT 35:
Mixing with Loops

WHAT is mixing with loops?

While understanding song structure is incredibly important, you may find that some of your songs have a short intro or lack a lengthy mixpoint. In the digital DJ era, we can easily set a loop to allow us to mix in and out easier.

WHY use a loop to mix?

Using a loop can be a great strategy if you are unsure of the length of the chorus. It can also be a great way to highlight a word or phrase when transitioning with wordplay.

There a few reasons for a DJ to use a loop in the mix:

Reason 1: Song B Has a Short Intro

By extending the intro of Song B, I can create a more seamless mix with Song A. This will help my audience hear a smoother transition between the two songs. (See Concept 21: Extending Intros.)

Reason 2: Song A Has a Short Mixpoint

Maybe there is a really short section that you want to mix out on. You can preset the loop to be able to extend that section while you mix in the intro of Song B.

Reason 3: Creative Mixing

There might be a section of Song A that has a particular phrase you want to create a loop around. While that section is looping, you bring in another song that has the same phrase, creating what is often referred to as a *wordplay* transition. Another option is looping a phrase from a song that was sampled by another song and playing both tracks back to back to help educate the audience.

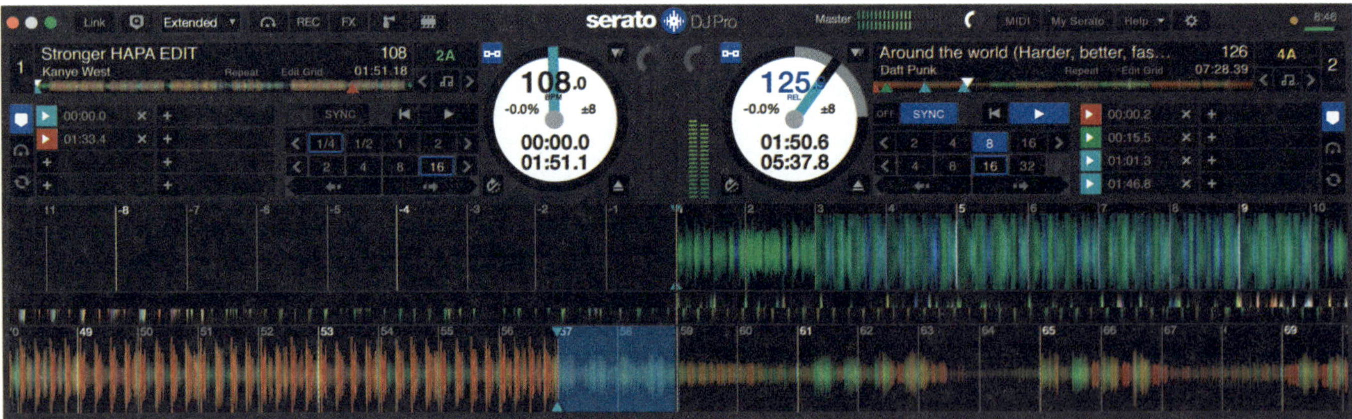

WHERE do I find the loop?

The loop is located in the software or on the controller under the section called "Loop." In the software, there is a section to adjust the length and activate the loop.

There are several places you can find the loop controls. On most DJ software, each deck has a set of loop controls. You will see that they have different loop lengths you can switch between.

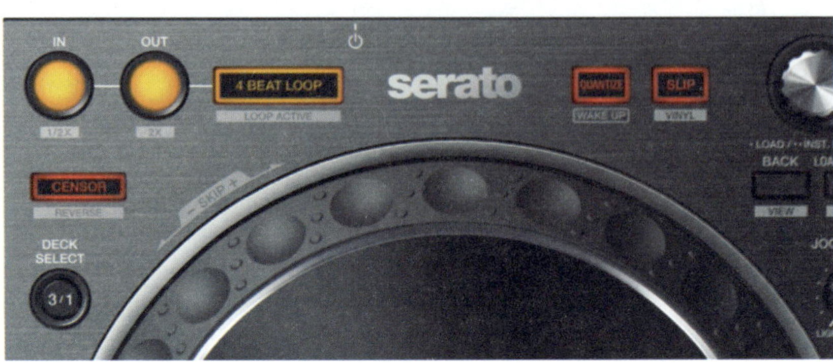

On the controller, there are several places where you can set a loop. If you want to set an Auto Loop, most controllers have a button that by default will set a 4-beat loop.

Some controllers have a knob that you can twist to select between the various loop lengths, and then push in the encoder knob to activate and deactivate the loop.

HOW do I mix with loops?
Here are a few suggestions for anyone trying to mix in or out with a loop:

Tip 1: Make sure the grid is correct.

If the grid is not correct, the Auto Loop will be set incorrectly and will make beat sync difficult. If you need to adjust the grid, be sure to do this before setting the loop. Also, make sure to zoom in close enough to the waveform to ensure the grid is correct. When zoomed out, the grid will often look accurate, but when you zoom in, you quickly realize it is incorrect. Even a grid that is 1/16 of a beat off will create problems when using a loop. (See Concept 17: Editing Grids.)

Tip 2: Try to preset your loops before performing.

While setting an Auto Loop during a performance is possible, a preset loop will be more accurate—and you can choose to use it or not when playing live. You can save these loops in most available DJ software. Some software even lets you set multiple loops and name them.

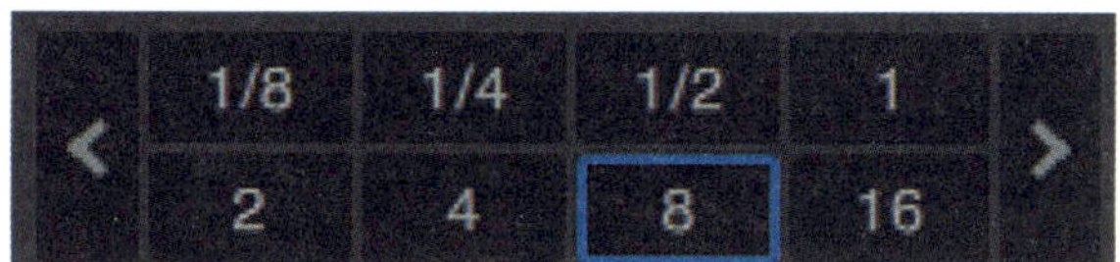

Tip 3: Make sure you learn the shortcuts for activating and deactivating the loops on the controller or in the software.

Loops can get away from a DJ fairly easily and if a loop plays too long, it will become jarring to the audience.

Related terms: loop, Loop Roll, Anatomy of the Mix

CONCEPT 36:
Recording

WHAT is recording?

Recording is the process of recording sound or performance for subsequent reproduction or broadcast. DJ software has the ability to record the master output of your performance so you can play back and listen to songs blending together, including any scratching, looping, and effects applied to your mix.

WHY is recording important?

Recording is an essential part of DJing. Although it can make DJs a bit anxious to record their performances, doing so provides the opportunity to listen back and acknowledge their progress. There have been many times when I thought a mix sounded good live, but upon listening back to it, I realized that Song B was too loud. Other times, thinking that a certain transition didn't feel good live, I listened back to it and actually liked what I did! In any case, listening back to your performances will make you aware of how you can improve your mixing and song selection.

In addition to what you can learn from your recordings, recording and uploading your sets is a great way to share your mixes with others. This will help to extend your brand and increase the public's awareness of your mixing style.

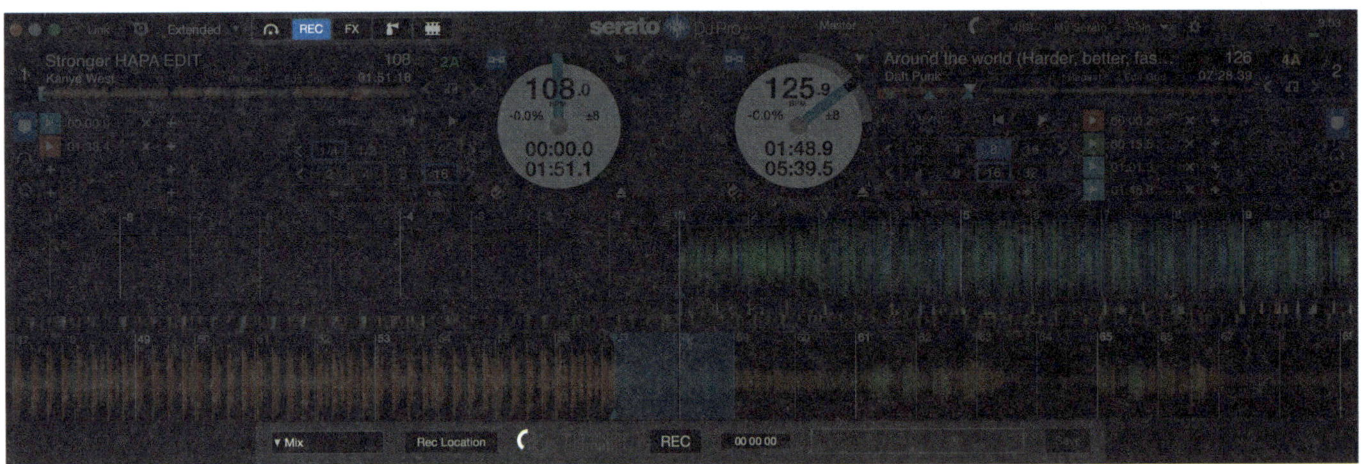

WHERE do I record?

In your DJ software, there should be a button that opens up a recording panel. There may also be several settings controlling the location in which the recordings will be stored. You can save the recordings to the default location or adjust the settings to save to a folder of your choosing.

Most DJ software will display an LED meter for the strength of the signal being recorded. It's crucial that the LED is not in the red when you are recording. This will create a distorted recording, and unfortunately there is no way to fix this. Because of this, most programs will record at a lower volume by default. The recording can be amplified later in another audio program if you wish.

Some recording panels include an option to record different sources. Just make sure that you are set to record the "master" or the "mix"; otherwise, you may be recording only one channel.

HOW do I improve my recordings?

Recording is a daunting psychological task for some, and you may find yourself getting nervous or not performing at your best. By continuing to record and listen back to the recordings, you will be able to analyze what you are doing correctly and what you need improvement on. I encourage you to record as much as you can. This will help desensitize you to the pressure you may initially feel.

In addition, when you listen back to your recordings, here are a few questions you can ask yourself:

- Were those two songs beatmatched?
- How was the volume during the transition?
- Was that a smooth blend?
- Do those songs sound good together?
- Do those songs have a similar energy?
- Did I mix out soon enough? Too soon?

Related terms: distortion, beatmatching

CONCEPT 37:
Vinyl Mode

WHAT is Vinyl mode?

In Vinyl mode, the controller's jog wheel behaves similarly to a vinyl turntable. When you touch and hold the top of the platter, the song will pause. Working the side of the platter will temporarily speed up or slow down the song. On most controllers, there is a button to toggle this mode on and off.

WHY is Vinyl mode important?

This is essential for any DJ that wants to rhythmically scratch on a controller (see Concept 48: Basic Scratching). It is also important for manual beatmatching techniques.

Since the DJ controller behaves like a vinyl turntable in this mode, it's a perfect way for DJs who are already familiar with the turntable to transition to the controller. It's also a way for DJs who start on a controller to familiarize themselves with the turntable, in case they come across a situation in which they need to perform on a turntable setup. This is certainly a possibility for club and bar DJs who may agree to a gig where the venue provides the DJ rig. In many of these cases, it is frowned upon and sometimes forbidden for a DJ to bring in his or her own rig. Instead, the DJ must perform on the rig that the venue provides. This is typically done when the venue spent money on their own system and has wired everything in the way they want it. They also have set levels for sound and amplifiers to fit with the preset rig, and they don't want to change those settings or risk having less than optimal sound for their venue.

WHERE is Vinyl mode?

As mentioned above, there is typically a button on the controller that will toggle this mode on and off. When toggled off, the track will stutter when hitting the Play/Pause button. This is meant to emulate some of the first CDJs (or CD players) that DJs used when compact discs were popular. The track would stutter when hitting the Pause button, and some DJs started to use this as an audio effect in their performances. Using the controller in this mode will also disable the ability to "hold" the track in place with your hand on the top of the platter. For these reasons, my recommendation is to toggle Vinyl mode on.

You can't scratch on the platter of this CDJ. This is just meant to temporarily speed up or slow down the song that is playing. This is the origin of "CDJ mode" and predates "Vinyl mode" on controllers and CDJs.

HOW do I use Vinyl mode?

There are quite a few benefits to using the controller in Vinyl mode. It can prepare you by building up your muscle memory for when you need to switch over to a vinyl turntable. Additionally, it gives you control of the song as you are bringing it in and gives you the ability to use scratching as a tool in your performance.

With Vinyl mode on, the temporary adjustments you make when manual beatmatching tend to mimic the way you would nudge and pull the track back on a vinyl turntable, with one exception. Most DJ controllers do not have motorized platters, whereas vinyl turntables do. Learning this adjustment to the "touch" and "feel" can take practice.

Vinyl mode takes the platter and divides it into two distinct parts that behave differently:

Part 1: Top of the Platter (marked as red)

By pressing down on it, you will pause the track that is playing. When you move your hand forward on it, it will behave as if it were a vinyl record. You could use this to rewind or fast forward the track as you press down on the top of the platter.

Part 2: Side of the Platter (marked as green)

This part is used for making minor adjustments to speed. By manipulating this part of the platter, you nudge the track ahead or temporarily slow it down by pulling backward in a counterclockwise direction. When doing this, the track will not stop but will be temporarily affected.

Related terms: scratching, manual beatmatching

CONCEPT 38:

Slip Mode

WHAT is Slip mode?

Slip mode is a feature that allows you to scratch, loop, or trigger cues during playback, while preserving the original playback of the track.

WHY is Slip mode important?

A more advanced mode, it can be used to add creative elements while not affecting the playback of the song. You can scratch a particular word while the track is still playing underneath on the same deck. When you release the part you are scratching, the track will pick up from where it would have been if you didn't start scratching. This can also be used to trigger a particular sound or sample in the current song by using Hot Cues.

WHERE is Slip mode?

The Slip mode button is usually located on the controller near the platter. It will likely blink when you engage Slip mode and are using a function in which the track is continuing to slip.

You can also turn on Slip mode in the DJ software. There are a variety of icons to indicate Slip mode, and this will vary depending on the software. When Slip mode is active, the icon may blink to alert you that Slip mode is engaged.

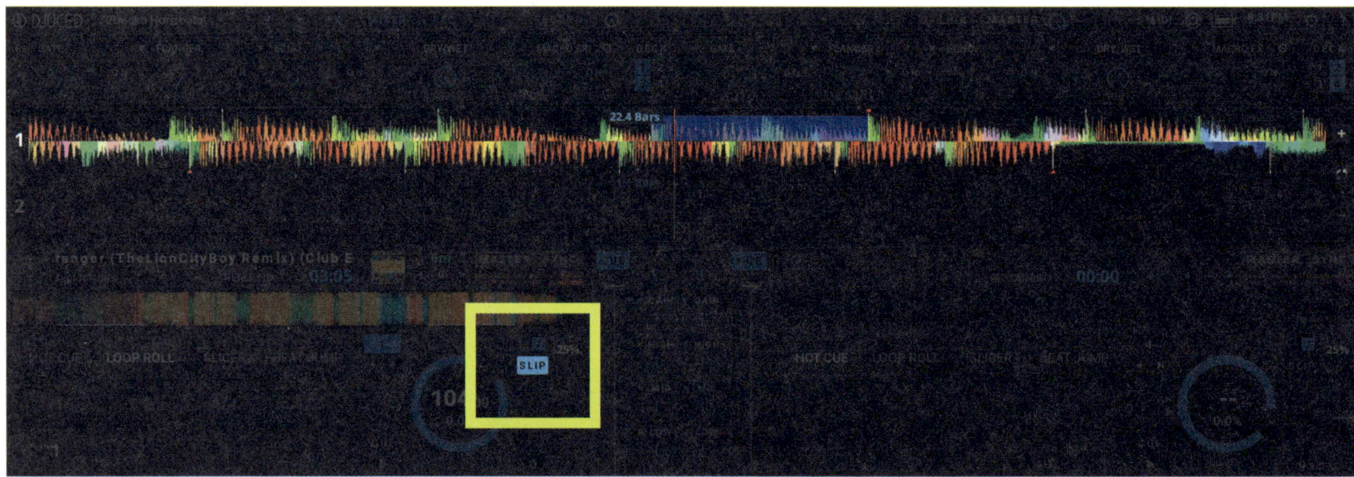

You may also see a moving playhead, which indicates how the song is continuing to play and where the playhead will be when you release the loop, Hot Cue, or sound that you are scratching.

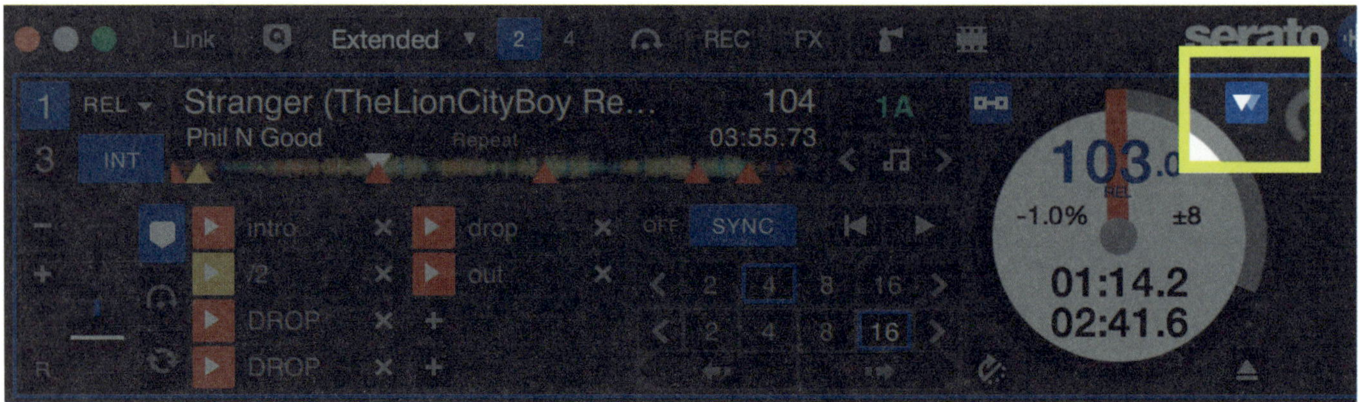

HOW do I use Slip mode?

It's important to know where this is located and how your controller and software behave when it is switched on. If you accidentally turn this mode on at a live gig, it may make you feel like an evil spirit has possessed your equipment! I would recommend practicing quite a bit with Slip mode before trying it live, as it can be disruptive to the audience if not executed well. A simplified version of Slip mode is using Loop Roll (see Concept 34: Loop Roll).

Let's look at one way that I would use Slip mode to take a sound effect from the beginning of a track and play it right before the chorus. In this example, I am going to use the vocal sample of "Yeah Yeah" that occurs right before the beginning of the first verse in Kendrick Lamar's "Humble." Keep in mind, this takes some preparation before performing it live.

Step 1: Set a cue point.

I have a light blue Hot Cue set to the "Yeah Yeah" sample.

Step 2: Identify where you would like to insert the Hot Cue.

I know that the chorus occurs from bars 17 to 25. It's an 8-bar chorus and I want to use the sample to sound like a call and response.

Step 3: Turn on Slip mode.

While the track is playing and before I get to bar 17, turn the Slip mode on.

Step 4: Execute.

Hold down the Hot Cue at the right point and then release it so the track keeps going with Slip mode on.

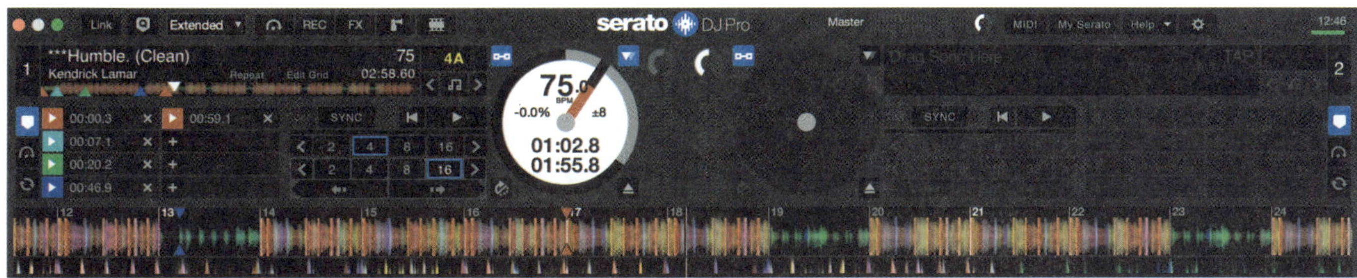

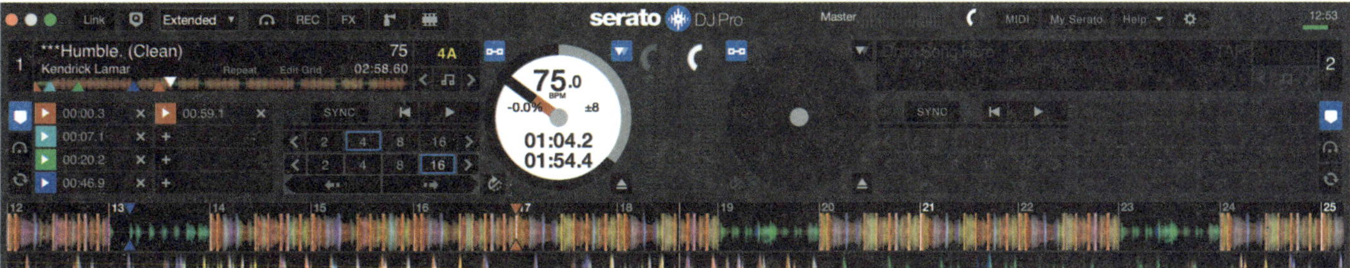

Step 5: Turn off Slip mode.

This is very important! Make sure to shut off the Slip mode so you can continue to mix in your next track without unexpected interruption from the Slip mode. (See video for Concept 17: Editing Grids.)

Related terms: scratching, Loop Roll, Hot Cues

CONCEPT 39:
Keyboard Shortcuts

WHAT are keyboard shortcuts?
Keyboard shortcuts are quick commands on the computer keyboard that activate functions in the software.

WHY are keyboard shortcuts important?
With any software, learning the keyboard shortcuts will help improve your accuracy and efficiency. With DJ software in particular, this is incredibly important as time is very valuable in performance. If you can save one second every time you load a song, that will add up very quickly. Also, there are some major limitations if you are trying to use the trackpad or the mouse.

WHERE are the keyboard shortcuts?
You can find a list of the keyboard shortcuts for your software in the Settings. Some programs like rekordbox and Traktor allow you to "teach" the software your shortcut preferences. Other programs like Serato DJ Pro have specific keyboard shortcuts that you have to memorize.

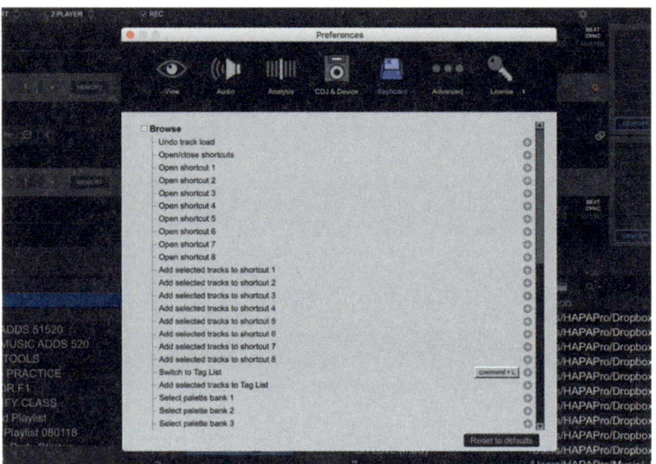

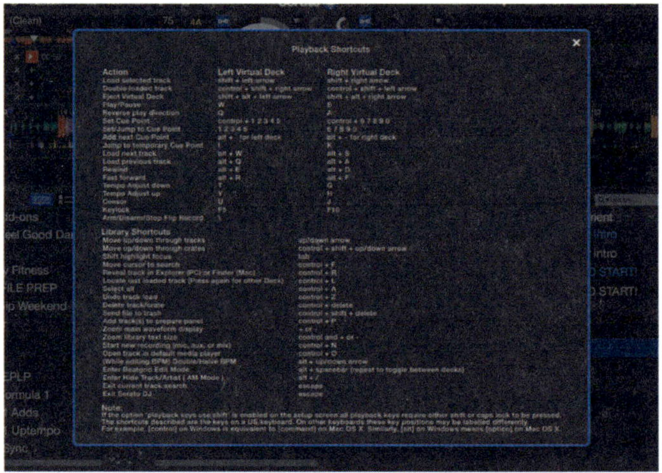

In Serato DJ Pro, you can click on the Help tab in the top-right corner and find a list of all the shortcuts. This can tend to be overwhelming, and some of these shortcuts you may never use. The top 10 keyboard shortcuts you will need are listed on the next page; however, another option is to purchase a keyboard cover that has the shortcuts printed on it.

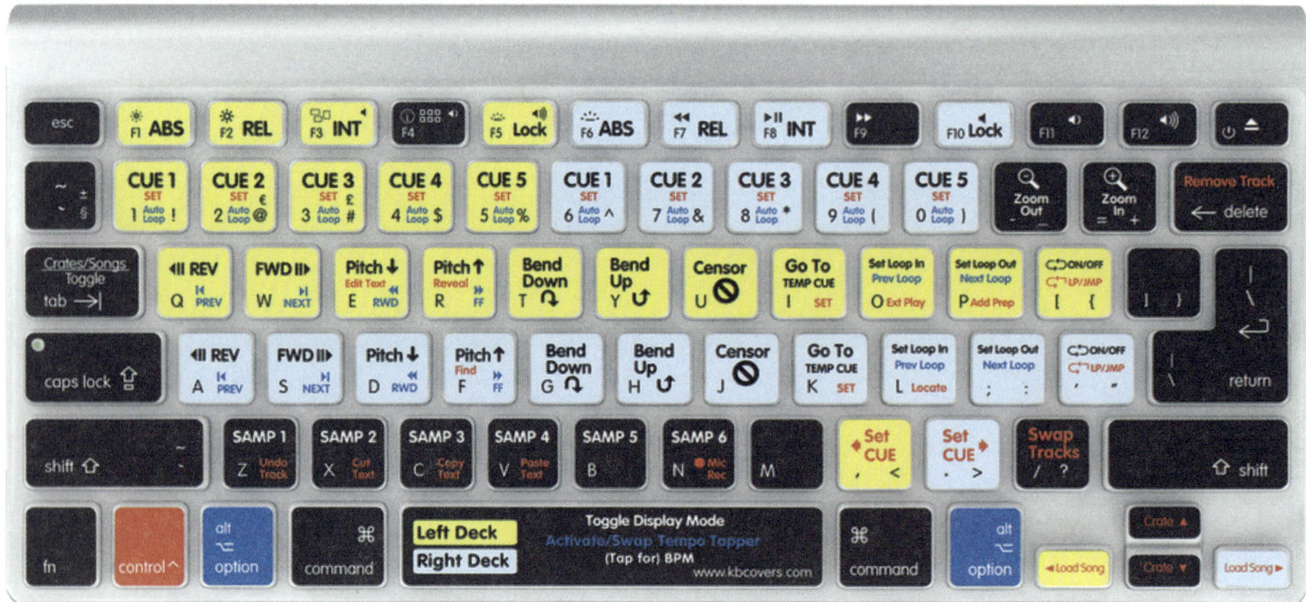

Some programs also have the ability to turn on a mode that shows you the shortcuts when you "mouse over" a function.

HOW do I use keyboard shortcuts?

I recommend not trying to memorize *all* the keyboard shortcuts. Think about the functions you use most and learn those shortcuts first. You probably use "Load Deck A" a lot and might still be painfully dragging the song from your browser to the deck. I would start there.

Keep in mind that many of the controllers are laid out with buttons or knobs that are also shortcuts in the software; however, you should still learn some of these keyboard commands for times when you are preparing files on your computer without your controller.

Some of the more popular and necessary keyboard shortcuts are:

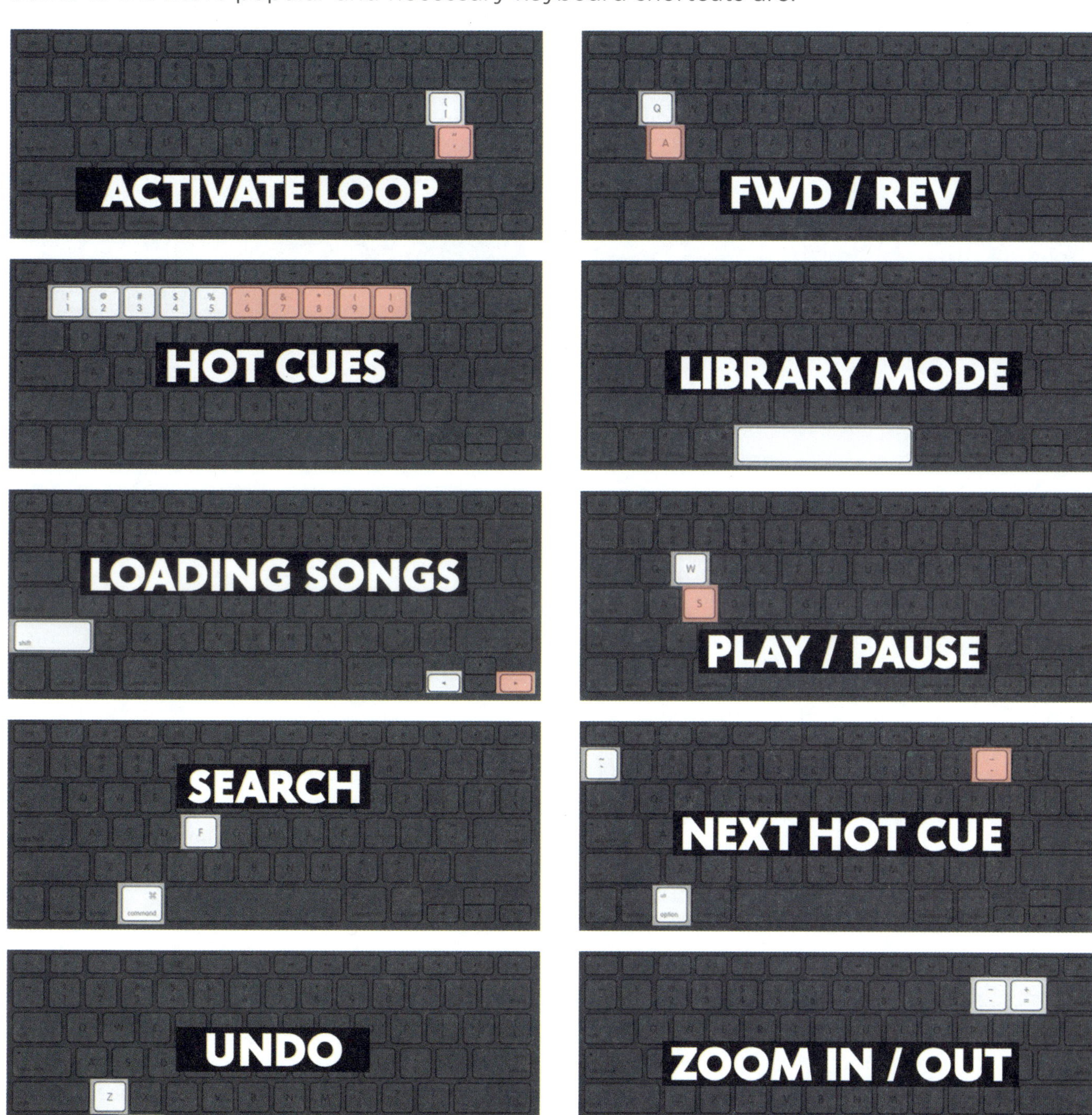

Related terms: software

CONCEPT 40:

Anatomy of the Mix

WHAT is Anatomy of the Mix?

After you have mapped out two songs (see Concept 3: Mapping Out Songs), you need to identify how you will get in and out of each song. The *Anatomy of the Mix* is an illustration of a typical blend where you have two songs simultaneously playing together for a specific number of bars and have identified the natural point of intersection.

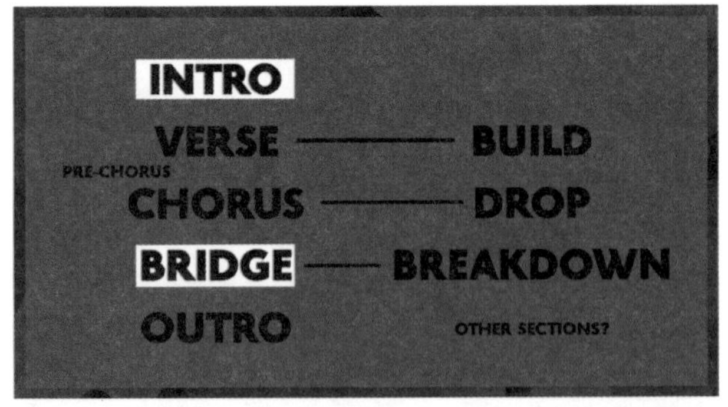

In the top image, I am identifying the In points on the left as either the Intro or Bridge.

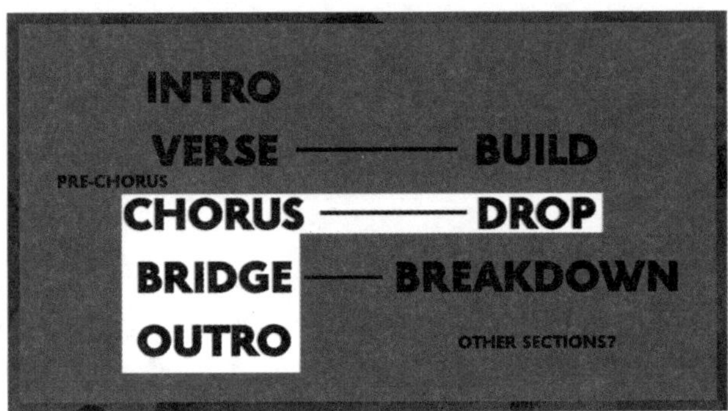

It's important to figure out where I am going to mix out of each song as well. Keep in mind that I am breaking down the song into its sections to understand how not to destroy it as I am mixing from one song to the next. I want to respect the original song structure and allow the song to get to one of its high points so the audience will feel satisfied before I change the song over.

WHY is Anatomy of the Mix important?

In an effort to maintain energy and nonstop music on the dancefloor, you need to make sure you fit the pieces of the puzzle together. This understanding of how to "close the gap" between songs and eliminate silence or unnecessary instrumental sections will determine your ability to continue feeding energy to the dancefloor. I like to think of the Anatomy of the Mix as the "box top" to a puzzle. You need to know what you are trying to achieve before you set out to do it. This vision will help you better understand how to execute the mix before you are in the middle of a performance and will give you more confidence as well.

WHEN do I apply Anatomy of the Mix?

We want to make sure to respect the songs that we are playing. As a DJ, we have the tools to completely manipulate, and in some cases, destroy the songs that we are using. I believe that part of the responsibility of the mixing DJ is to find ways to enhance the musical experience for your audience, and one way to do this is to switch songs before they carry on too long. A part of the DJ's job is to understand how long is too long. This comes from being able to read your crowd and pick up on nonverbal cues.

After mapping out the songs, you should know where the high points are. For most popular songs, this would be a chorus, or possibly a bridge. Our role is to make sure we deliver at least one of those high points to the audience before changing the song over. And when we do change the song over, it should enhance the experience by being a perfectly blended transition to another song of similar vibe and energy, and of course, one that holds a similar tempo for the dancefloor.

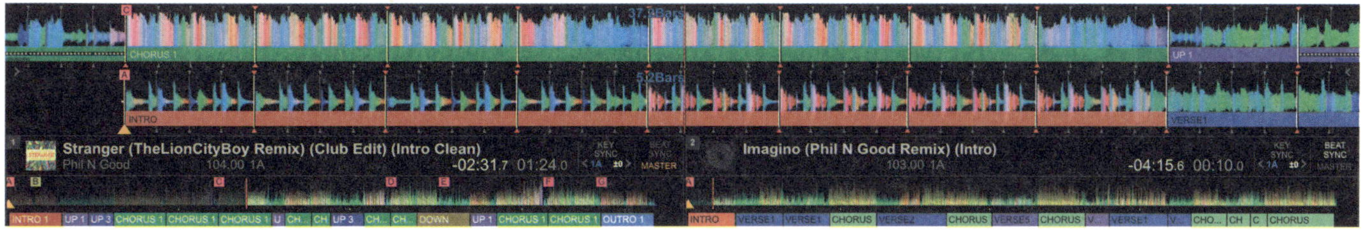

HOW do I apply Anatomy of the Mix?

Once you have identified your mixpoint sections for Song A and your mix-in length for Song B, you can set Hot Cues. These Hot Cues can help you understand how long those sections are. When the chorus of Song A and the instrumental intro of Song B are the same lengths, transitioning between tracks will be easy. You simply start the intro of Song B at the beginning of the chorus of Song A and they will finish at the same time, producing a perfect mix.

In some cases, they will not be the same length. For instance, what if Song A has an 8-bar chorus and Song B has a 4-bar instrumental intro? When would I start Song B?

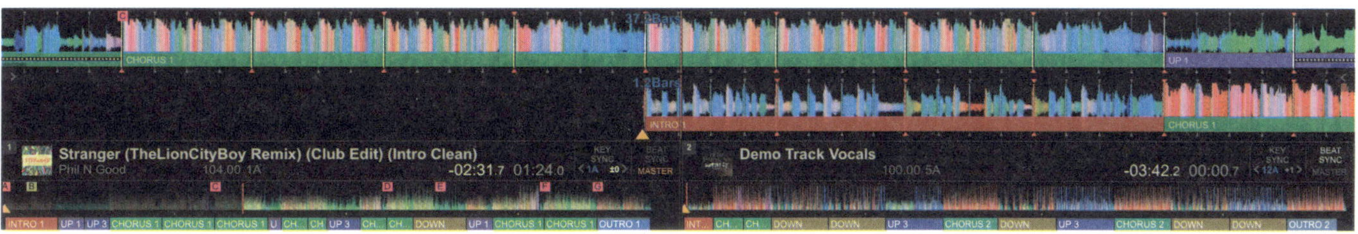

We want to start Song B halfway through the chorus, so that both phrases end at the same time. It's not as important that they are the same length. What matters more is that they end at the same time. For example, if Song C has a 2-beat intro, where would I start that?

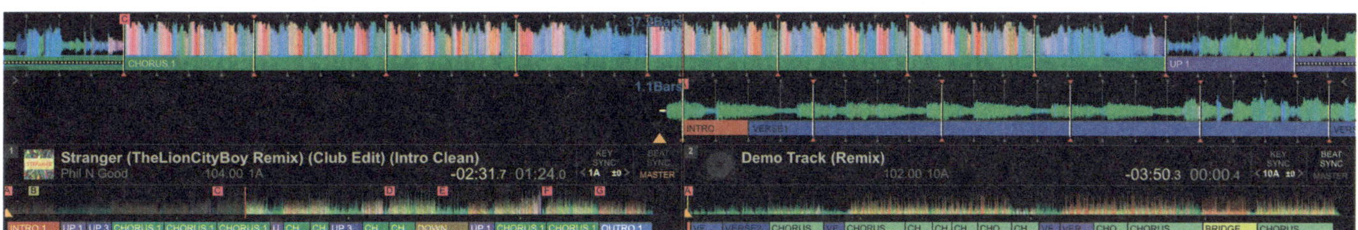

We would start Song C 2 beats before the end of the chorus. We would start it on the third beat of the 8th bar, so that the end of the phrase lines up.

Understanding this Anatomy of the Mix is a critical part of perfecting mixing as a DJ.

Related terms: cue, pre-cue, headphones

CONCEPT 41:

Organization Part 1—Library Backup

WHAT is a library backup?

This is a safe and seamless way to have a backup file of your tracks, playlists, and any other important information in your DJ library.

WHY is a library backup important?

Software crashes. Computers fail. Hard drives get corrupted. These things happen—it's not a matter of "if" but "when." You will have spent a lot of time and energy gathering music from different sources, mapping out your songs, setting Hot Cues, and tagging your tracks. Personally, I would rather lose a safe of cash than lose my DJ library.

WHERE should I back up my library?

I would recommend against using physical hard drives. Instead, I would use a cloud service. Any physical drive can fail. Plus, it takes a lot of time to plug in the physical drives and back things up every time you get home from a gig. I used to do this, and I still have at least a dozen 1TB hard drives lying around my house—most of which have the same content on them—and I rarely ever pull them out.

I converted everything to Dropbox and *love* the ability to "Selective Sync" and keep files organized and securely backed up in the cloud. I also keep the files I need on my laptop, and whenever I edit a song (even by just adding a Hot Cue), Dropbox recognizes that I made a change and as soon as I am connected to WiFi, it automatically syncs up to the cloud to ensure that everything is current and up to date!

There are lots of other options beside Dropbox, and I encourage you to find what works best for you. Here are some considerations when looking for a good backup and organization system:

- Sync functionality
- Cross device (desktop, mobile, web)
- Cross platform (Mac and Windows, Android and iOS)
- Ease of use
- Price
- Storage capacity

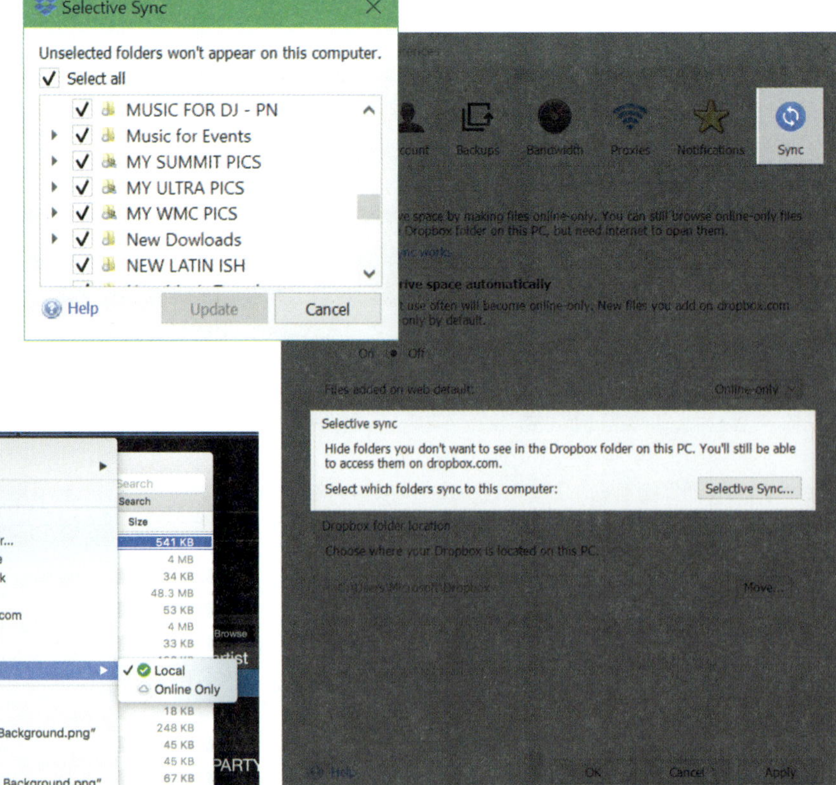

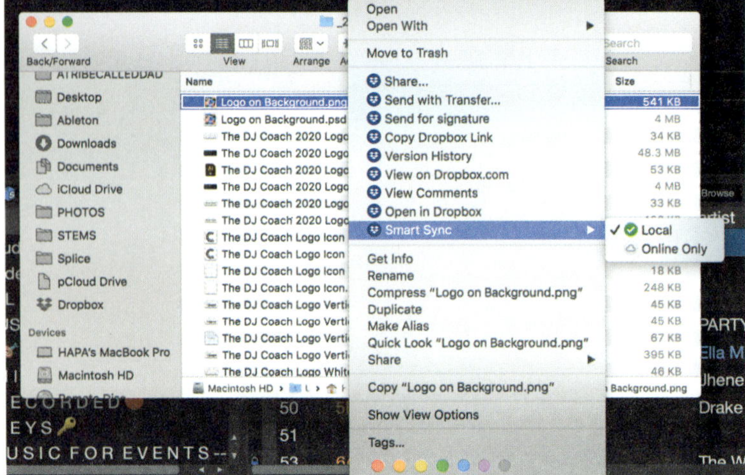

HOW do I back up my library?

If you take my advice (and I hope you do), you just need to move your music folders into a Dropbox folder. This will then act as a "super folder" and will keep everything inside that folder in sync with the music on your computer. If you no longer want a file to take up space on your computer, just uncheck the status of "Local" in the Selective Sync options and it will be removed from your computer—but still stored safely in the cloud for when you need it.

I use this feature especially for music that I download for gigs with a specific theme—music that I may not want taking up space on my computer on a daily basis. Holiday parties, movie premieres, roaring '20s parties are all great examples of this.

In your DJ software, the structure of your playlists and the database will be backed up as well in either your "Documents" or "Music" folder. Your software may prompt you at the end of each session on whether you wish to back up. Do it. If it doesn't prompt you, it is likely already backing itself up automatically (though this varies with different programs).

Here's a quick step-by-step guide of my process for downloading, organizing, and backing up music, leveraging the power of Dropbox Selective Sync:

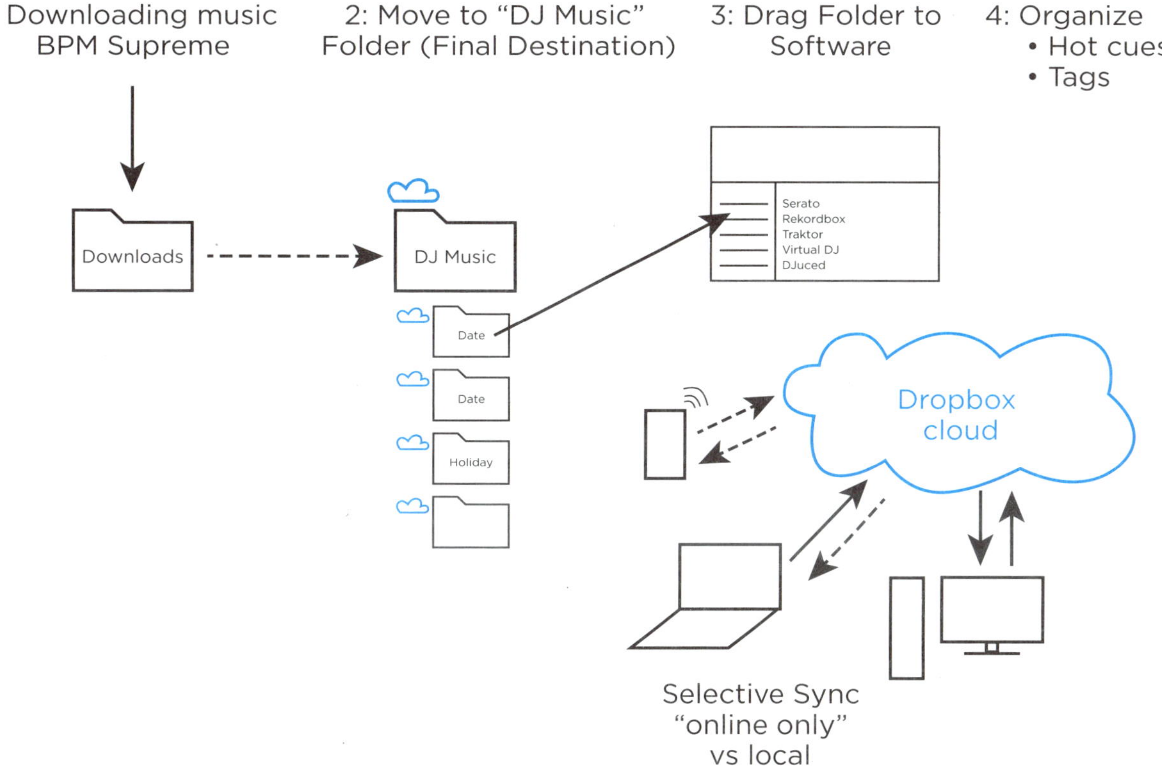

Step 1: Download music. I have kept the default location so when I download new songs, they go into my "Downloads" folder.

Step 2: Move songs to "DJ Music" folder. One of the reasons I don't download directly to this folder is that if I download music, photos, videos, or anything else non-DJ related, it will also end up in this folder. Now that I have downloaded the music that I want, I move it to a "DJ Music" folder, which is already located inside a Dropbox folder. Anything in that folder will automatically be backed up to the Dropbox cloud.

Step 3: Import the music to my DJ software. Now that the music is where it should live, essentially forever, I can bring it into my DJ software.

Step 4: Organize my music and tag it. Using my own organization system, I can tag a song based on genre, mood, instrumentation, or whatever else I choose. I can put this song into multiple crates or playlists, or I can have the system help me by tapping into the Smart Crates or Intelligent Playlists. (See Concept 42: Organization Part 2—Playlists.)

Related terms: software, playlists

CONCEPT 42:

Organization Part 2—Playlists

WHAT are playlists?

Most of us are already familiar with a playlist as a way of organizing our music collection. Playlists break up this large group of songs into digestible folders that can be organized by genre, mood, or any parameter you wish. DJ playlists expand on that concept. Within playlists, you can have sub-playlists and organize the various columns to sort by BPM, Key, Genre, Label, Year, and so on.

There are also playlists referred to as Intelligent Playlists or Smart Crates. Within these playlists, you can set specific parameters and the DJ software will scour your library and instantly populate a playlist based on your wishes.

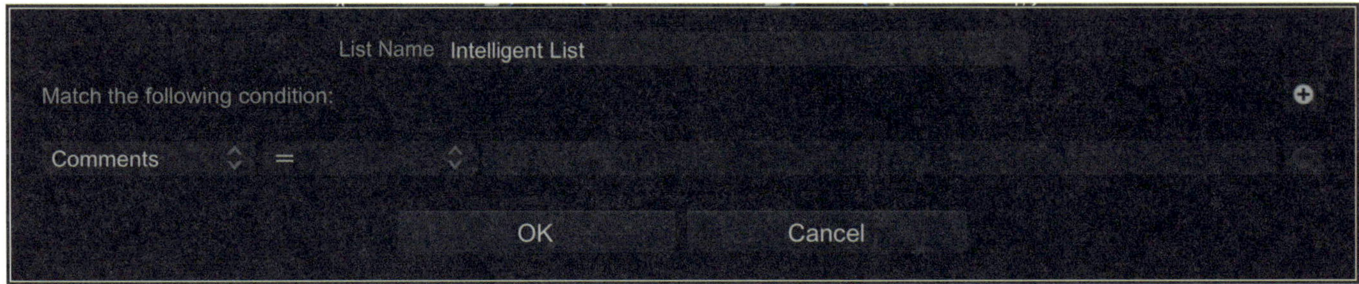

WHY are playlists important?

Organization is crucial in the digital DJ era. Before the digitization of music, DJs had far less music to choose from when building their music library. An impressive DJ library in the 1990s was 800–1000 vinyl records. Even at that point, there was no way a DJ would play all those songs in a given night. Now, most DJs have 10 times that much music in their hard drives. With all this music, organization is incredibly important for knowing what songs are in your library and accessing those songs quickly and easily.

When grouping songs together, I get a better understanding of which songs may *sound* good together. The last thing I want in the middle of a performance is to feel stuck, not knowing which song I should play next. At the same time, I also don't want to just follow a pre-planned set verbatim. Playlists create a middle ground between these extremes.

WHERE do I create playlists?

In the browser section of the DJ software, on the left-hand side, you will see options to create a playlist or crate. Start thinking about how you want to organize your music. I have gone through several iterations of playlist organization, and it's always a work in progress.

I am a big fan of creating sub-crates or playlists within folders. In my current system, I have a main folder called "Move." Within that folder, I have playlists or sub-crates around particular vibes, genres, or tempos. This helps me in a live scenario when I am trying to manage a dancefloor. Anything in that folder should be a song that is danceable. On the contrary, I have another main folder called "Vibe." Inside of Vibe, there are sub-crates or folders around particular genres and tempos. If I am playing at an art gallery opening, or something that isn't a dancefloor, I will go to this main folder or any of the sub-crates and find the appropriate music.

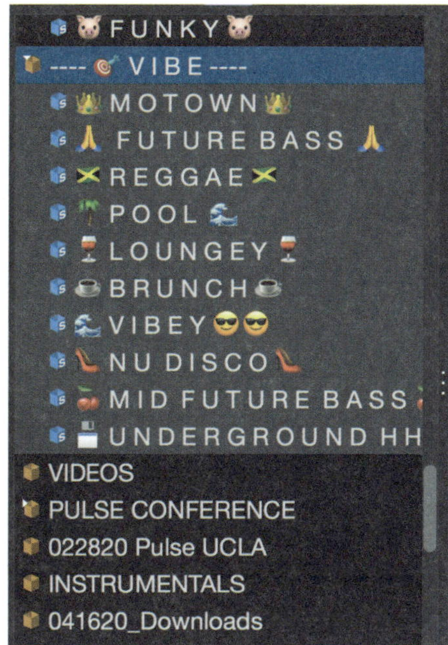

HOW do I create a Smart Crate?

Intelligent Playlists or Smart Crates can help automate a lot of this work for you over time. I can create a Smart Crate called "Vibe," and every time I tag a song as "Vibe" in the comment field, I can set a rule to move that song into the "Vibe" Smart Crate. One of the best things about this is that you can have multiple tags on files, and they can live in multiple crates or playlists without being a duplicate file.

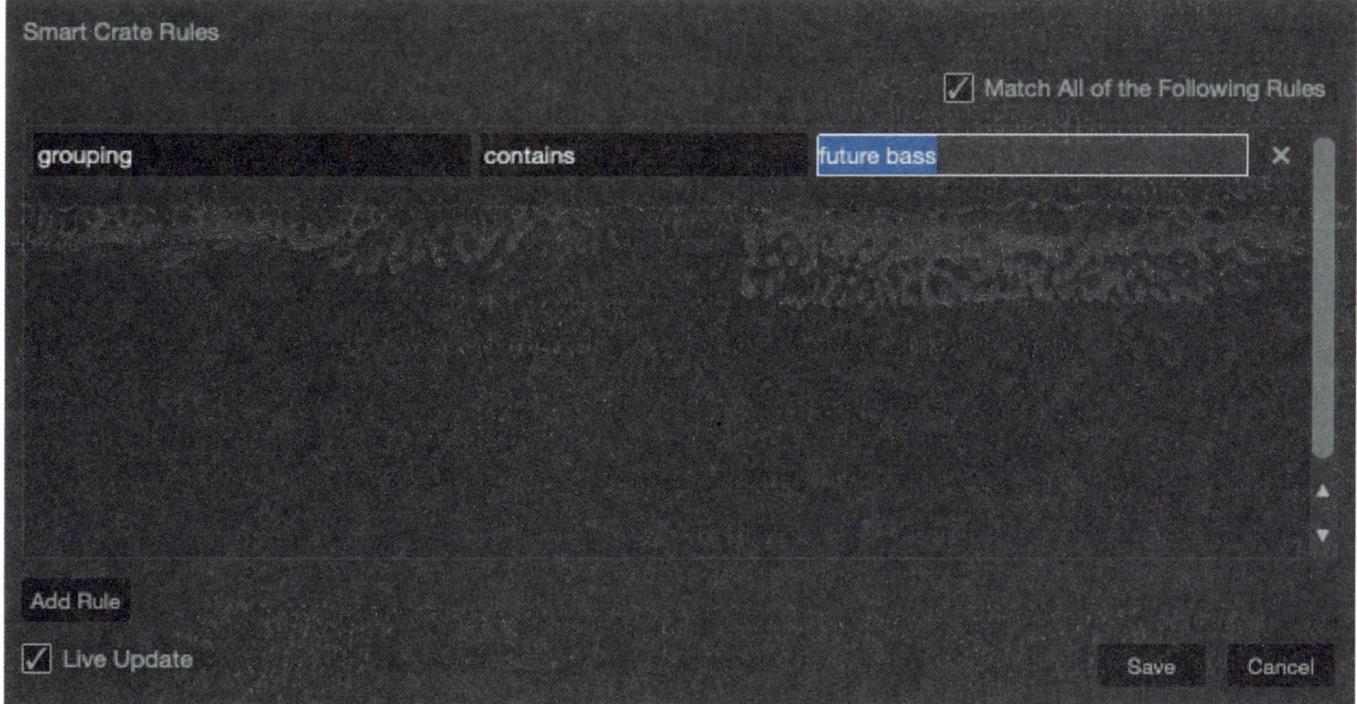

Related terms: software, crates

CONCEPT 43:

Instant Doubles Mode

WHAT is Instant Doubles mode?

When this setting is checked on, it allows you to copy the song on Deck A and put it seamlessly in play on Deck B.

Instant Doubles allows you to match the playhead position of two tracks. With this option set, when you load the same track on one virtual deck that is already loaded on the other virtual deck, the playhead will jump to the position of the track that was loaded first.

WHY is Instant Doubles mode important?

Instant Doubles mode allows you to essentially DJ off of one deck, while still maintaining the ability to mix. This is particularly important when troubleshooting—especially when using your software with vinyl turntables, which can have issues that prevent the software from reading properly (needles, bad RCA cables, broken tonearm, etc.).

Instant Doubles mode also allows you to start beat juggling, using identical records on each turntable. Likewise, it allows you to manipulate two or more samples, drumbeats, or vocals using pauses, scratching, backspins, and delays.

WHERE do I find Instant Doubles mode?

In most software, you need to select this mode in Settings or Preferences. Once you have enabled the mode, you should be able to simply drag and drop the song that is playing on one of the virtual decks and it will pick up at the current playhead automatically. There are also keyboard shortcuts for this mode and even an Instant Doubles feature on many controllers near the Load Track button.

Load	Load Setting ☐ Playback starts at Memory/Hot Cue nearest to the beginning of the track ☑ Instant Doubles
	Load Method ○ Load Button ○ Rotary Selector (Push)

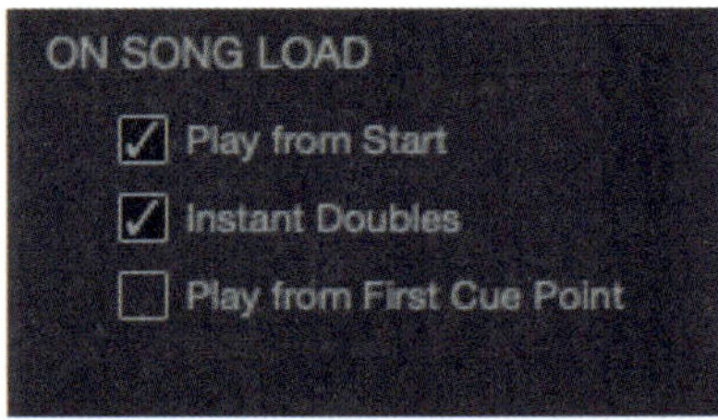

HOW do I use Instant Doubles?

For DJs who are using the DVS function with vinyl turntables and timecode control vinyl—or CDJs and timecode control CDs—it is possible to run into a live scenario in which one of the decks is not functioning properly. In this situation, understanding how to use the Instant Doubles feature can save the day, or night! Here's how you would do it:

Step 1: Check Settings.

Make sure the mode is switched on in Settings/Preferences. I would advise you to just keep it checked on. It won't do anything if you aren't actually using it, and this way, when you need it, you won't have to dig back into the Settings panel in the middle of a live performance.

Step 2: Identify which deck is working.

Let's say only the left deck is working in this scenario, so we will need to make the right side our internal, or virtual, deck.

Step 3: Make the non-working deck virtual.

Set the right deck to INT mode (Internal mode).

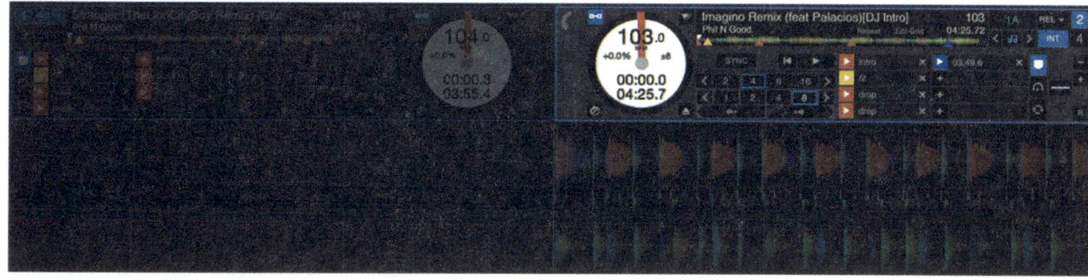

Step 4: Play Song A on the left deck.

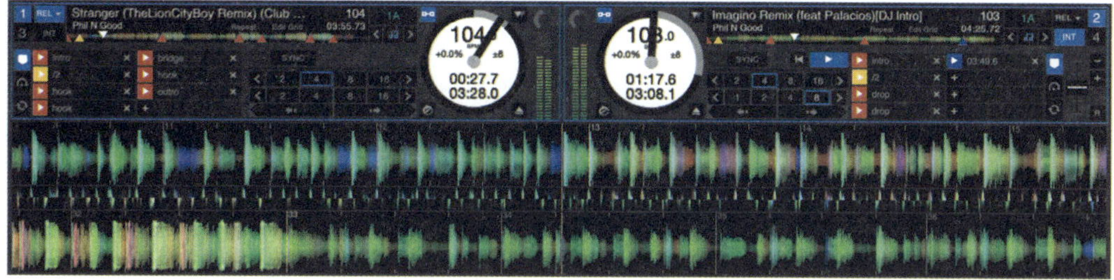

Step 5: Copy Song A onto the right deck.

You can do this by either dragging and dropping the song from deck to deck or by using a keyboard shortcut. Some mixers also have an option to double-tap the Load button to duplicate the song onto the virtual deck.

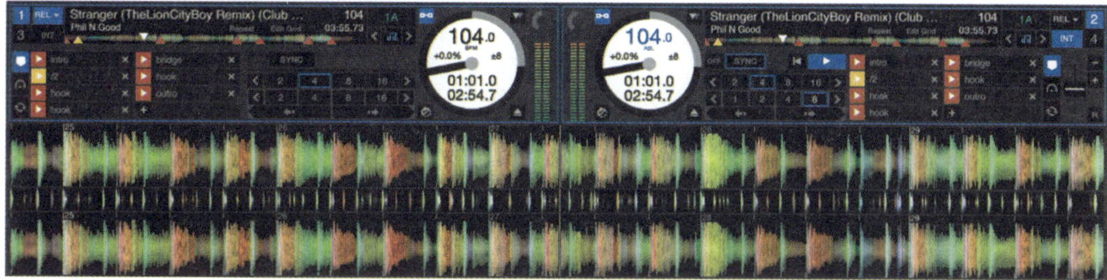

Step 6: Quickly change the crossfader over to the right side.

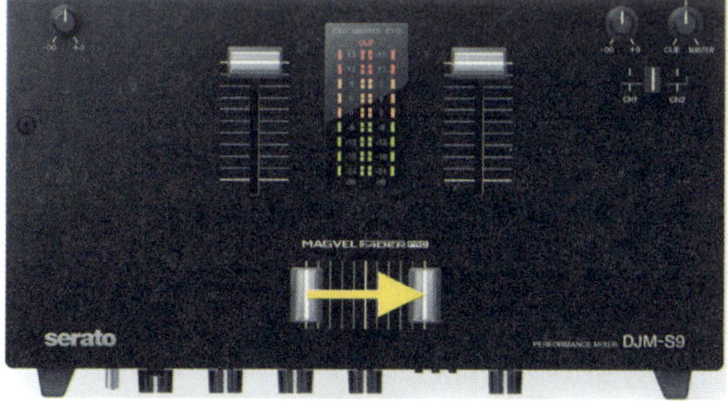

Step 7: Load up Song B on the left deck and mix it into Song A.

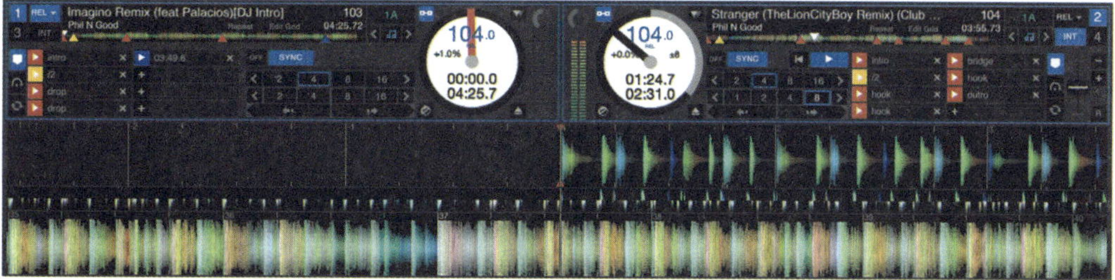

Step 8: Repeat! Keep that going all night if you have to!

This is an essential skill to practice, especially for DJs who are on turntables. It has less of a use when on a controller, but it is still helpful if for some reason you want to free up the deck that the track is currently playing on. I tend to practice this way at least once a month, so I'm accustomed to it when faced with an issue in a live scenario. Technically, I really only need one turntable to play all night!

Related terms: software

CONCEPT 44:

Faders

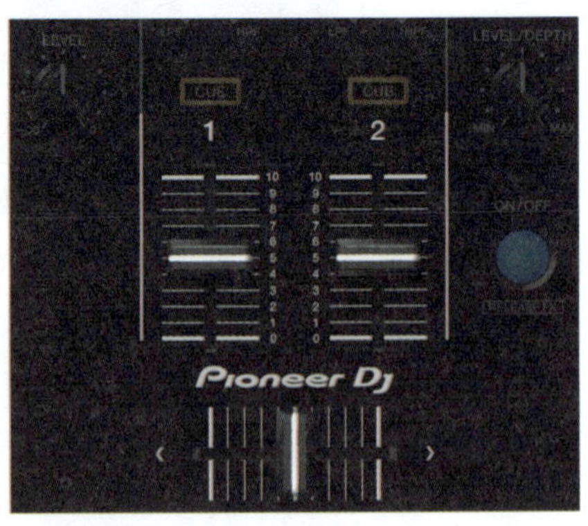

WHAT are faders?

There are two basic types of faders on a DJ mixer or controller: *channel faders* and a *crossfader*.

WHY are faders important?

The channel fader allows the DJ to control the volume of the designated channel. Most channel faders go from 0 to 10. Being able to slowly raise and lower the volume is incredibly important in creating a seamless mix from Song A to Song B.

The crossfader functions a bit differently from the channel faders. The crossfader was originally designed to automatically crossfade between two sources. Let's say we have Song A on the left side and Song B on the right. When the crossfader is all the way over to the left, we are just hearing Song A. When the crossfader is all the way to the right, we are just hearing Song B. And technically, when we are in the middle, we are hearing an equal 50% of Song A and 50% of Song B.

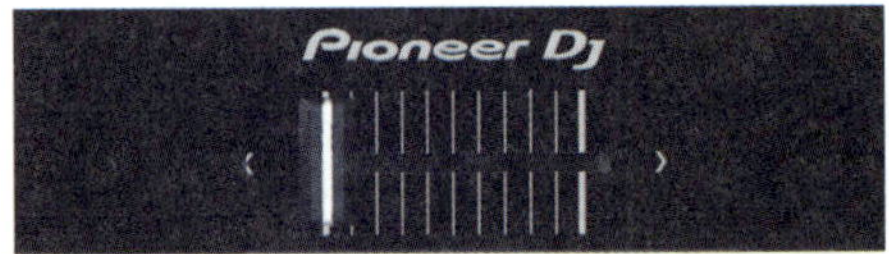

WHERE are the fader settings?

On some hardware, you will find a crossfader Curve setting. This will change the behavior of the crossfader. The setting that resembles an "X" is usually the default Curve setting, which will produce the effect of bringing both channel volumes down to 50% when the crossfader is in the middle. When you move from the middle of the crossfader to the right side in this setting, the percentages of volume of Song A and B change proportionally (e.g., 3/4 to the left = 75% of Song A and 25% of Song B).

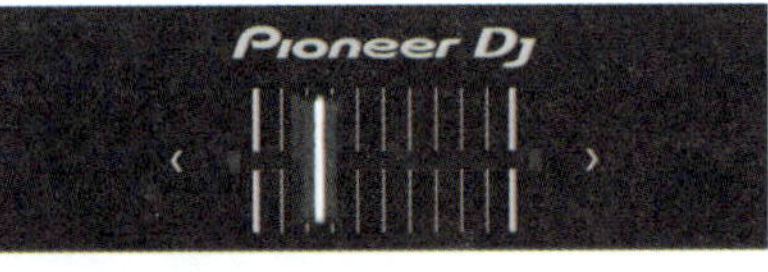

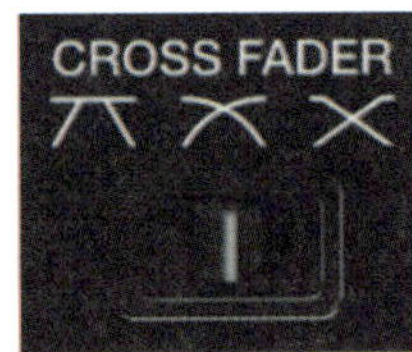

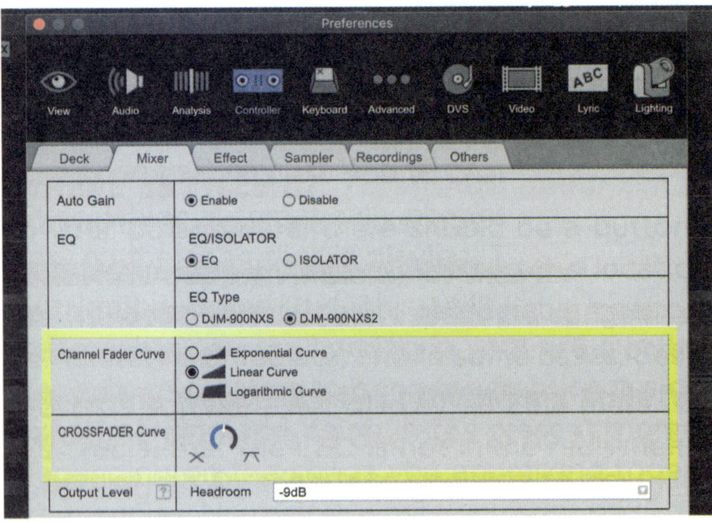

In some cases, there is not a physical switch to toggle between on the hardware and this setting is controlled from the Preferences section in the software.

There may also be a setting for the channel faders as well.

HOW do I use faders?

I like to set my crossfader to "cut." This setting has the shape that looks like a picnic table and eliminates the gradual fading between Song A and Song B with the crossfader. For that purpose, I like to use the channel faders; I feel like I have a lot more control over the volume and sound this way. For instance, what if I wanted 100% of Song A and only 50% of Song B? I couldn't achieve that on just the crossfader. I would need to use the channel faders.

Here are a few steps for using the faders when mixing Song A and Song B together:

Step 1: Make sure the channel fader for Song A is all the way up.

I don't want to have to match volume on the channel fader by trying to get Song B to 8.2 or something. That would be very difficult. If there is a difference in volume, I can use the Trim or Gain to give that channel a volume boost.

Step 2: Set the crossfader in the middle.

Since my crossfader is also set to "cut," I don't have to worry about where the crossfader is precisely positioned, just as long as it is not all the way to one side or the other. Anywhere in the middle will produce the same sound.

Step 3: Start to fade up Song B.

When it's time, I will start Song B. After it's playing, I will begin to increase the volume by raising the channel fader. About halfway through the chorus, I am usually all the way to the top of the channel with the fader.

Step 4: Use the EQ or Filter.

(See Concept 32: Smoothing Out the Mix.)

Step 5: Lower the volume on Song A.

At the end of the chorus, fade out using the channel fader for Song A.

Important note:

I am not moving both channel faders at the same time. I am bringing Song B's channel fader up to the top before bringing Song A's channel fader down.

Related terms: software

CONCEPT 45:

Virtual Decks

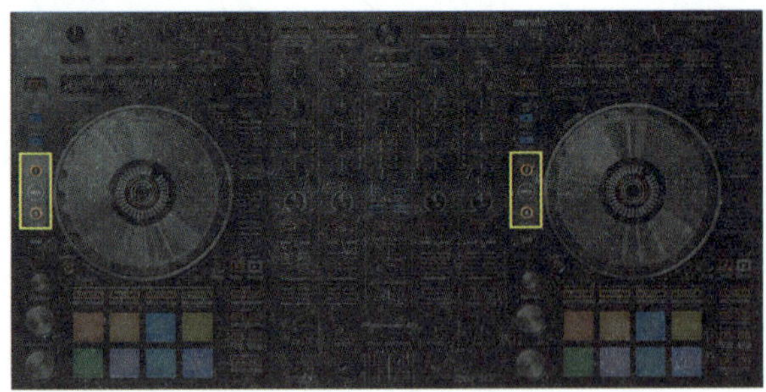

WHAT are virtual decks?

In your DJ software, you probably have the ability to play up to four songs at the same time. You may have a DJ controller that has four channels; however, Decks 3 and 4 are virtual decks that share a platter and performance pads with Decks 1 and 2.

WHY are virtual decks important?

Once you have gotten the hang of controlling two songs, it may be helpful to explore your creativity and try mixing three or four songs or pieces of audio together. Keep in mind that this can get a little confusing, so make sure you have two decks down before you start incorporating Decks 3 and 4.

The awareness of this capability is also great for troubleshooting. There have been times when I have accidentally hit the toggle button for Deck 3 and couldn't figure out why I couldn't control the song that was playing on Deck 1.

WHERE are the virtual decks?

There is typically a button on the controller that will enable Deck 3 and a separate button to enable Deck 4. Decks 1 and 3 share the same "left" side, and Decks 2 and 4 are on the "right" side. Once you enable one of the virtual decks, the platter and performance pads will then control that deck.

HOW do I use virtual decks?

Let's say I was going to mix three songs together using Decks 1, 2, and 3 on a Serato DJ Pro-compatible DDJ-SX3. This controller has four channels and will allow me to control volume and EQ on my virtual decks, even when I cannot use the performance pads or the platter.

Step 1: Start playing Song A on Deck 1 and bring the volume fader up.

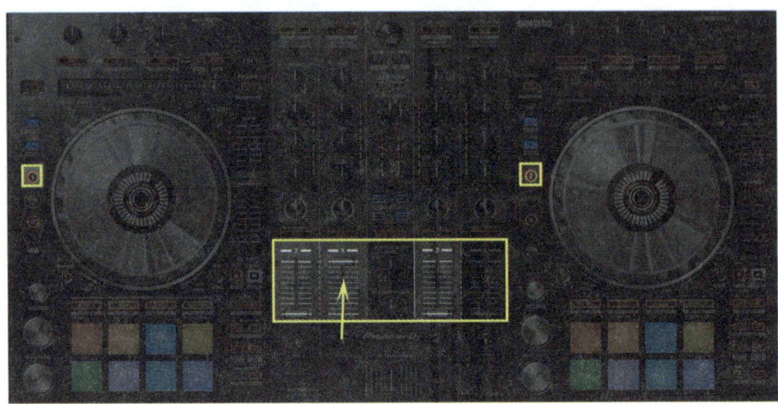

Step 2: Mix in Song B on Deck 2 and bring the volume fader up.
Now I have two songs playing together in sync.

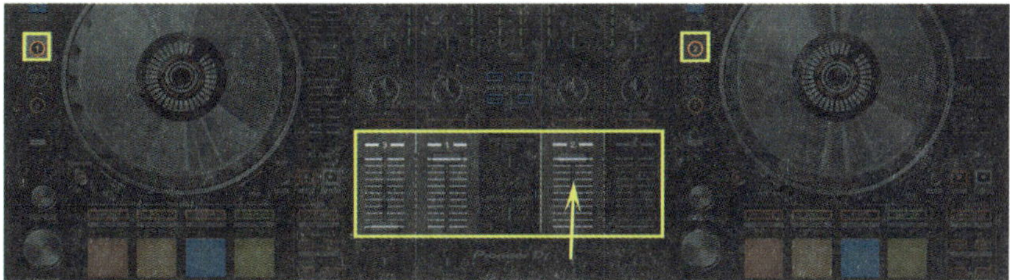

Step 3: Hit the Deck 3 button.
My platter and performance pads are now reserved for Deck 3; however, I can still control the volume and EQ for Deck 1 in the mixer section of the controller.

Step 4: Mix in Deck 3 and bring the volume fader up.
Now I have three songs playing at the same time.

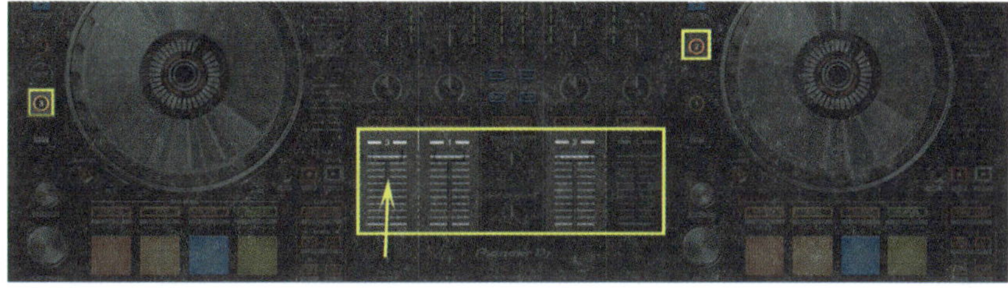

Step 5: Switch back to Deck 1 by toggling the Deck 3 button.
Now the platter and performance pads are reserved for Deck 1 again.

Step 6: Set a loop out of Song A on Deck 1 and fade it out.

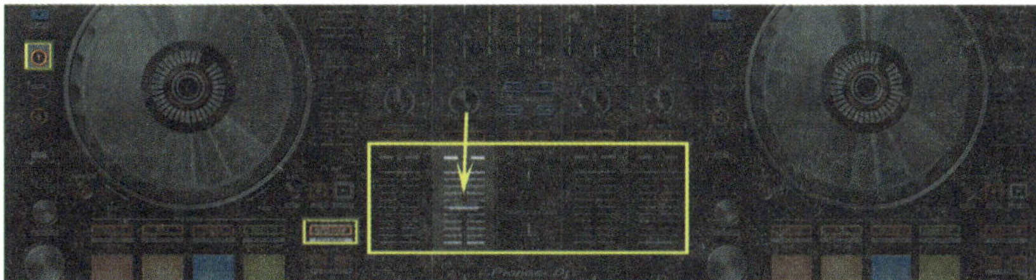

Again, this can be a bit complicated, so be sure to get comfortable mixing two songs together before adding in three or four decks. Trying to mix four songs together can be super challenging, as there's quite a lot of sound going on, but it can be incredibly fun and can help you explore your creative ideas as a DJ!

Related terms: software

CONCEPT 46:

CDJ

WHAT is a CDJ?

CDJ stands for Compact Disc Jockey, and this media player was made popular by Pioneer DJ. DJing evolved from vinyl records and turntables to digital CDs and compact disc players. These first CDJs behaved similarly to the commercial CD players at the time but also had the ability to set a temporary cue point and change the tempo of a song to allow DJs to mix.

Since then, the CDJ has certainly evolved. The modern-day CDJ has a computer inside it and a full-color touchscreen display allowing DJs to set Hot Cues, set loops, alter keys, and beat jump—while also having the ability to sort through music files stored on SD cards, USB drives, and more.

WHY is the CDJ important?

The CDJ has become the industry standard on festival stages and in nightclubs around the world. With the flexibility of being stand-alone players but also having the ability to work in HID mode or with timecode control CDs, CDJs are used by DJs with many different types of preferences. Learning on CDJs can be challenging for the average beginner, as the cost of each CDJ is about $2000 USD! So if you were to have the full rig with two CDJs and a mixer at home, you would be looking to invest about $6000 USD.

Learning how to use CDJs is important for many DJs that aspire to work in nightclubs and on festival stages throughout the world. Thankfully, CDJs work well with rekordbox and many other software platforms, so getting acclimated isn't too difficult.

WHERE do I find CDJs to learn on?

Since price can be a barrier to getting started, some DJs end up renting CDJs for a weekend to get acquainted with them. There are also less expensive media players and controllers that work similarly to the coveted CDJ-2000NXS2 flagship, such as XDJ-RX, XDJ-1000, and CDJ-900NXS players. These options can be a fraction of the price yet still work off the same software, and they are laid out in a similar fashion since they are produced by the same manufacturer, Pioneer DJ.

Other players have also entered the market, like the Denon DJ Prime 4 and Engine Prime series of products. These behave similarly to the CDJ setup but with some different features. (See Concept 13: Choosing a Rig and Concept 14: Choosing DJ Software.)

HOW do I get started on CDJs?

The most natural way to use CDJs is with the rekordbox software, which you can download free at rekordbox.com. After that, you can use the software to organize your music and then export your tracks to a USB drive, which you can then stick into the CDJ. If the CDJs are linked together with a CAT5 Ethernet cable, you only need to have one USB drive—although I recommend making a copy of the USB drive just in case.

It's really important to note that the DJ fundamentals will transfer from any rig to any other rig. Try not to get overwhelmed when looking at new equipment. I like to use the analogy of getting into a rental car. Even though this may not be the same make and model as the car you own, you should be able to drive it off the lot. It may take you a moment to get used to where certain functions are, but that won't inhibit you from being able to drive. You would likely look for the most necessary functions first—same with the DJ equipment. In a rental car, I don't necessarily need to know where the seat warmers are in the middle of July. On the DJ equipment, I wouldn't necessarily need to know where the Loop Roll button is right away.

CONCEPT 47:
HID Mode

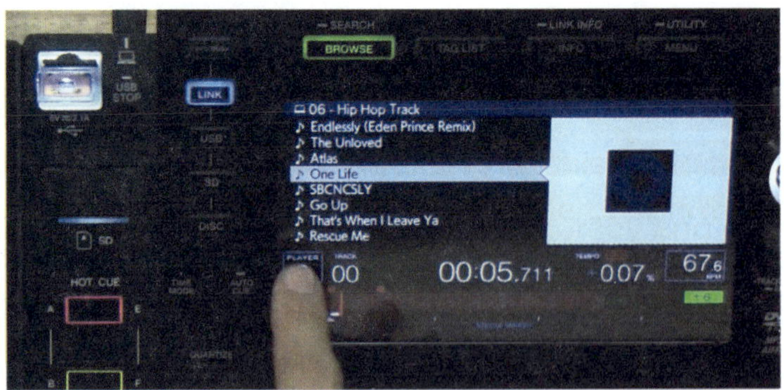

WHAT is HID mode?

HID (or human interface device) mode transforms a CDJ. From a device merely playing DVS timecode for your DJ software, HID turns your CDJ into a full-featured controller with the ability to trigger Hot Cues, set loops, and more. It also adds information to the CDJ screen including waveforms, BPM readout, and the ability to search the library from your computer.

WHY is HID mode important?

There are several great uses for HID mode:

Reason 1: There is no need for timecode to control CDs or files.

By plugging directly from the back of the CDJ to your computer, you can eliminate the need to carry around timecode control CDs.

Reason 2: It unlocks features on the CDJ and makes it more convenient.

Sure, you can hit your laptop keyboard shortcut to trigger the first Hot Cue on the left deck, but wouldn't it be better to have that right on the CDJ itself?

Reason 3: It turns the display screen on the CDJ into a functioning display.

You can look through your library, view the waveform, and get the BPM information right on the screen. You can also toggle between crates and playlists and select your songs right from the CDJ itself.

WHERE do I enable HID mode?

HID mode can be turned on by following these steps:

Step 1: Make sure to connect the CDJ to your laptop via USB cable.

This is not for the USB on the top of the CDJ, but instead from the back of it. This is USB A to USB B.

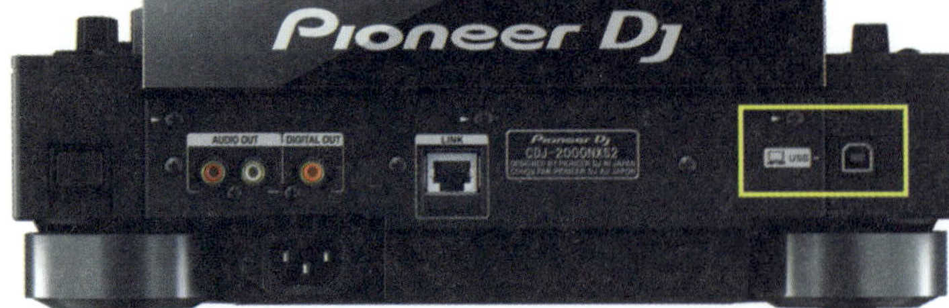

Step 2: Click on Link on the CDJ.

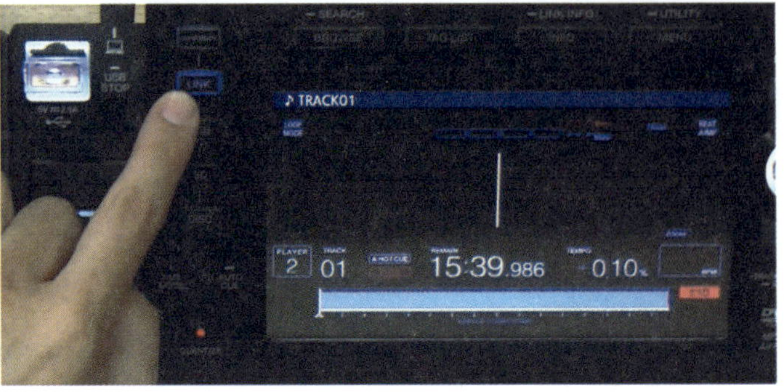

Step 3: Click on Control USB.

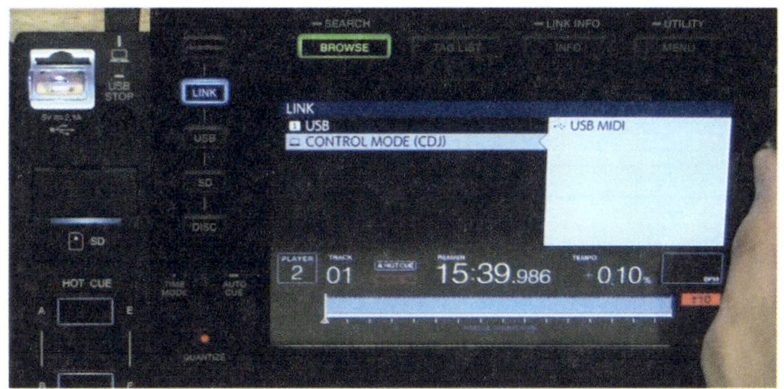

Step 4: Push in the Encoder button.

Step 5: Select which deck you wish to control.

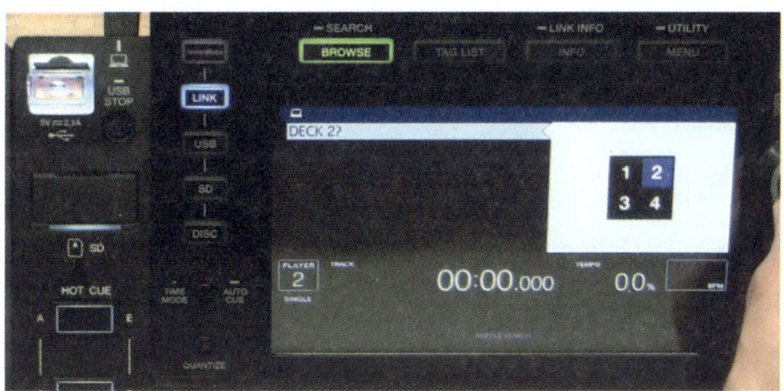

HOW do I connect HID mode?

Outside of the steps listed above, there are a few things to keep in mind.

HID mode requires a USB cable for each CDJ. Depending on your laptop, you may not have enough USB ports (because the actual mixer or audio interface is connected via USB as well). For example, in order to have two CDJs using HID mode with Serato DJ Pro, you will need three USB ports.

For some DJs, that will require you to have an additional USB hub. It is important that the USB hub is powered.

Also, when you are using HID Mode, your Serato decks should be in INT or Internal mode. The CDJs are now acting like MIDI controllers instead of media players. This means you can also disconnect the RCA cables running from the CDJ to the mixer, because you are technically not sending any audio into the mixer from the CDJ.

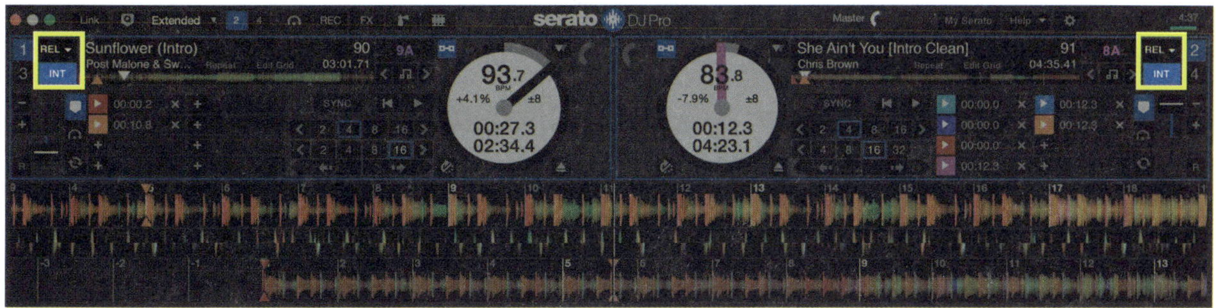

CONCEPT 48:
Basic Scratching

WHAT is basic scratching?

Scratching is using the turntable or DJ platter in a manner similar to a percussion instrument. Scratching can be used as an accent to a song that is already playing or can be used to introduce a song before releasing it on the deck. Scratching can demonstrate to the audience a sense of control that the DJ possesses.

WHY is basic scratching important?

Reason 1: Control

Learning how to scratch can teach you control. This control is great for mixing as well as just scratching. As you begin to understand the mechanics of scratching, you will have a greater understanding of the turntable or DJ controller as an instrument.

Reason 2: Adding Texture

Scratching a particular vocal or instrument sound—like a horn stab—can add texture to a song if done appropriately. Scratching can tend to get a bad rap, and that stems from audiences hearing non-rhythmic scratching noises that can be piercing to the ear and distract from the music. The key is to be able to use the scratch to enhance the musicscape.

Reason 3: Improved Timing

Related to control, when you practice basic scratching, your overall rhythm and timing will improve. This will drastically improve your ability to drop songs on the "1" in time.

Reason 4: Switching Up the Tempo

Learning how to mix is fundamental, but so is being able to switch up the tempo. Learning some basic scratching can help with what could be an awkward transition. (See Concept 31: Changing Tempo.)

WHERE do I scratch?

Bringing in a song:

When preparing to bring in a new song, cue up right before the first downbeat or "1." If you move your hand back and forth slightly, you shouldn't really hear anything, but as soon as you bring your hand forward, you should hear the beat (possibly a kick drum). Practice bringing the sound backward and forward so that it sounds consistent.

Adding texture to a song:

Find a vocal sound that complements the song that is playing. Cue up to the beginning of that sound. Find an open section in the song that is playing, maybe an instrumental section on the bridge or a long intro. Create rhythmic patterns with the sound by moving the platter forward and backward with your fingers pushing down on the platter. When ready, you can remove your fingers from the platter to let the sound play. Then, rewind it back to the beginning of the sound to repeat if you wish.

HOW do I scratch?

Here are some tips for basic scratching:

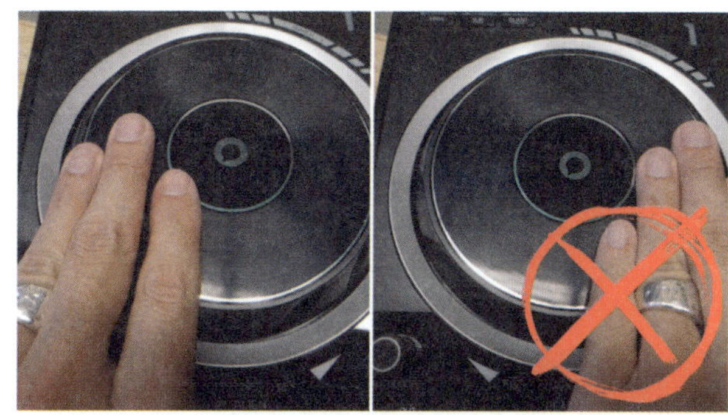

Tip 1: Look at the platter like an old school clock. When you are cued up to the beginning of the sound, readjust your hand on the platter so that you are at 9 o'clock, which will be your starting position. You should be bringing your hand, with the platter, back to 9 o'clock.

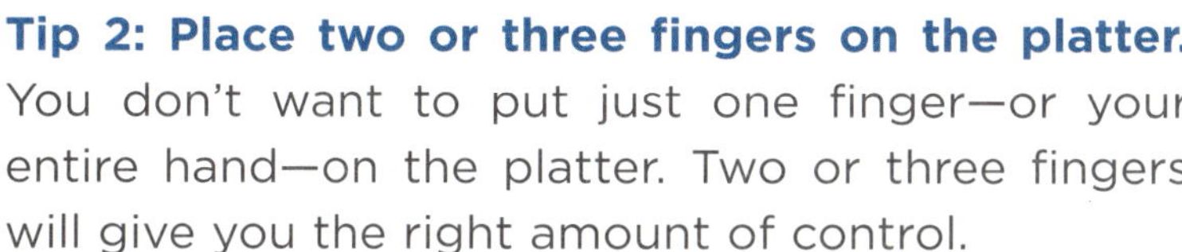

Tip 2: Place two or three fingers on the platter. You don't want to put just one finger—or your entire hand—on the platter. Two or three fingers will give you the right amount of control.

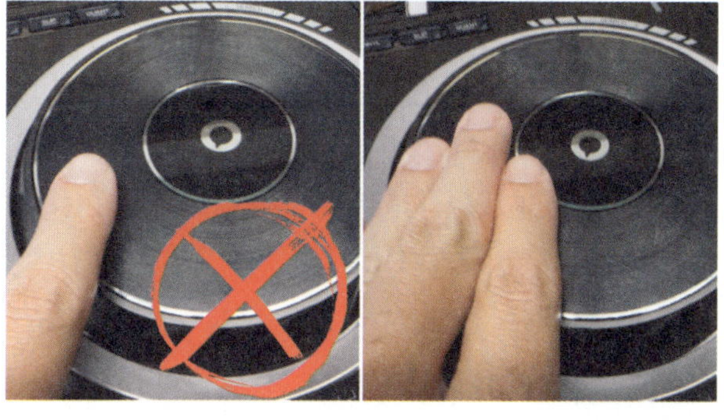

Tip 3: Use a full arm motion. It's really important that you don't move just your fingers or just your wrist. A full arm motion will help create a consistent sound.

Tip 4: Use your body! Move to the music that you are scratching along to. Bob your head, tap your foot, or dance so you can keep your scratching in rhythm.

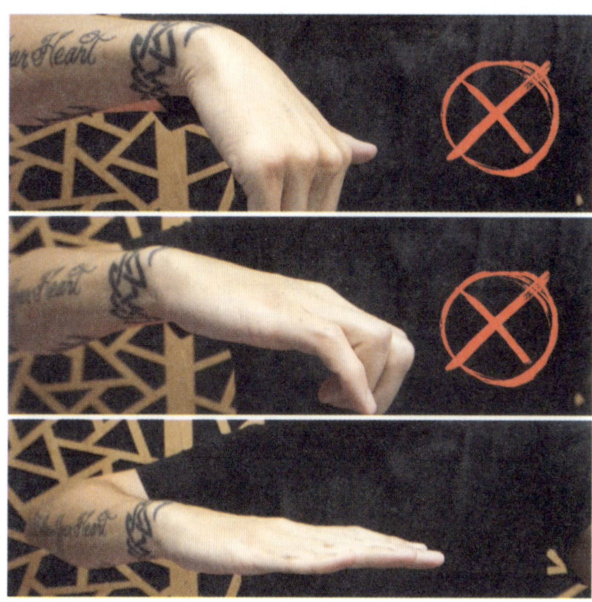

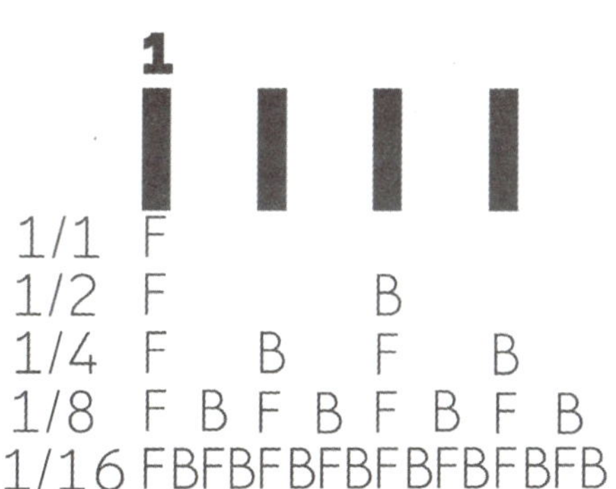

F = Forward / B = Backward

These are the same notes you would apply to other instruments as well. Some of you who are already familiar with basic music theory—but not structure—may recognize this as:

Whole note (semibreve)

1/2 note (minim)

1/4 note (crotchet)

1/8 note (quaver)

1/16 note (semiquaver)

BONUS AUDIO TRACKS In addition to all of the videos, this book also comes with two audio tracks containing special scratching loops you can use. Visit *www.halleonard.com/mylibrary* and enter the code found on page 1 to access them!

CONCEPT 49:

Sampler

WHAT is Sampler mode?

Sampler mode opens up a panel where you can launch one-shot samples and loops to enhance your DJ performance. This can also be expanded and used as a way to create beats on the fly, using the performance pads on a DJ controller.

WHY is Sampler mode important?

Sampler mode is not a crucial part of DJ performance, but it can add extra texture and layers. Most commonly, this mode is used to play one-shot sounds on top of your mix. You may have heard a DJ playing a siren or an air horn on top of a brand-new song. DJs will also have a custom-created "drop," or "tag," they can play during sets to identify themselves. A famous example of this is DJ Khaled being heard on virtually every track he has produced.

In Sampler mode, you can also use a percussive sound to enhance a particular moment in the track by filling in something that is missing. For instance, maybe there is a section of Song A that goes to a breakdown and all the drums come out of the original track. You could cue up a kick and snare on the sampler and play the drums over that section to fill it in!

The sampler can also be used for loops. By triggering different loops on the various sample slots, you can essentially start to create your own beat.

WHERE do I find Sampler mode?

By default, the Sampler mode is hidden. The panel can be accessed in the software, and it will open up a section with slots for you to load samples into. There is also a set of parameters for each sample, including volume and behavior of the sample.

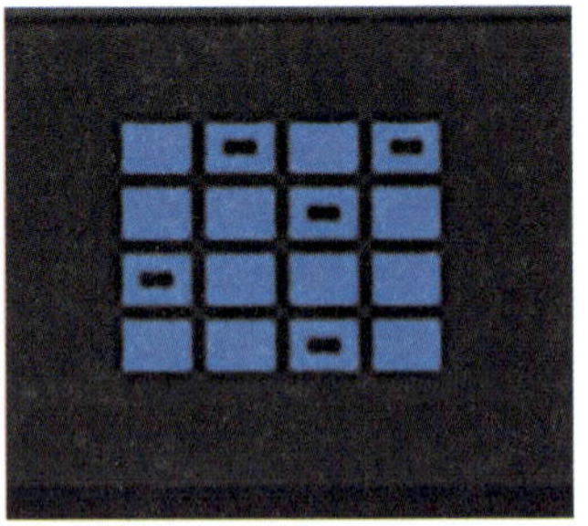

On most DJ controllers, there is a separate mode that will transform the eight performance pads into sampler slots. Look for the tab on the controller, above the performance pads.

HOW do I find sounds for the sampler?
There are lots of different sources for samples:

- Sounds (Native Instruments)
- Splice
- Loopmasters

sounds.com

In addition, a simple Google search will likely pull up quite a few options.

In terms of being able to create your own DJ drops and imaging, check out Fiverr.com, which can be a great source for creative freelancers all over the world—including voice-over artists who specialize in this!

CONCEPT 50:

Quantize

WHAT is Quantize?

Quantize mode will snap your actions and timing to a beat grid, according to the parameter of your choosing. Say you set Quantize at 1 beat. When you hit a Hot Cue but you are not exactly on the beat, Quantize will correct the inaccuracy and lock in the Hot Cue according to the beat grid, exactly *on* the beat. Quantize mode is perfect for DJs who use *drum cues* (see Scenario 3 below) or need to be on point when jumping through sections of a track.

WHY is Quantize important?

Here are a couple of scenarios in which enabling Quantize mode would be helpful:

Scenario 1: Setting Hot Cues Quickly

When I prepare a track and am getting ready to set Hot Cues, I enable a 1-beat Quantize to ensure that my cues are snapped to the beat grid and are not slightly before or after the beat.

Scenario 2: Jumping to a Particular Section in the Song with or without a Hot Cue

With a 1-beat Quantize on, you can jump to a section of the song—and even if you blindly hit the waveform, the track will stay on beat since Quantize is enabled.

Scenario 3: Cue Point Drumming

This is a more intermediate/advanced skill. If you wanted to ensure that your timing was perfect while creating a drum pattern, you would enable Quantize mode and maybe set the parameter to be 1/4 beat instead of 1 beat.

WHERE do I find Quantize settings?

The Quantize parameter settings are located in your software's Preferences.

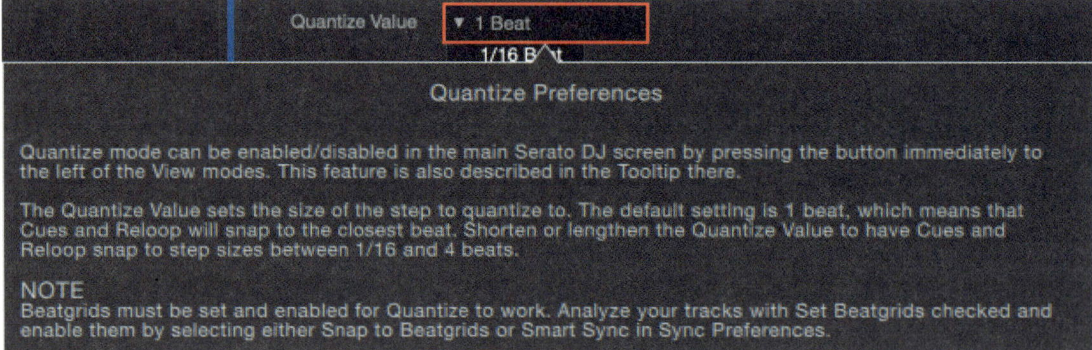

You may be able to enable Quantize on each deck or on the full rig, depending on the software and hardware you are using. Quantize is usually indicated by a "Q."

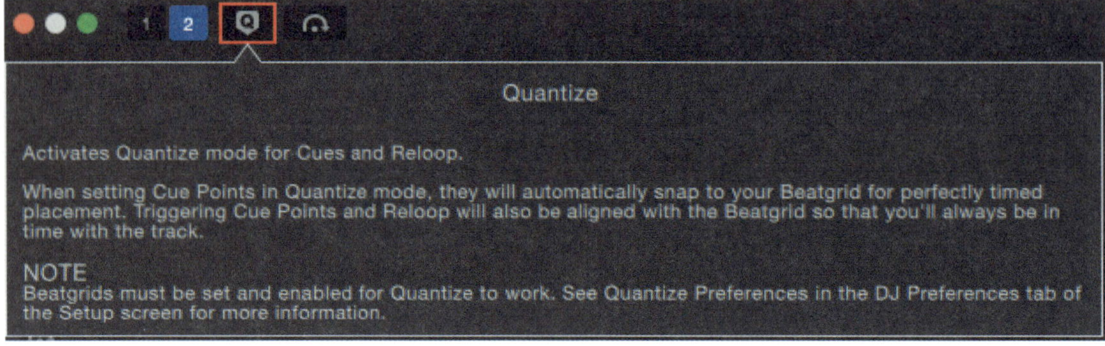

Quantize:
When the Quantize function is turned on, cue and loop points are automatically set to the nearest beat position. You can select the basic value for quantize in [Preferences].

HOW do I use Quantize?

It's pretty simple. Turn it on when you need it, and be sure to turn it off when you don't. I usually only have Quantize on when I am preparing songs and prefer to have it off when performing. This gives me a little added pressure to have to hit the Hot Cues on beat; it also gives the performance a bit more of a human feel. On that note, I want to encourage you to embrace the "imperfection." Some of my best sets were not planned. As creatives, we strive for perfection that seems to be ever elusive. That's what continues to push me and keeps me going all these years later. (For more on Quantize, see video for Concept 19: Hot Cue Strategy.)

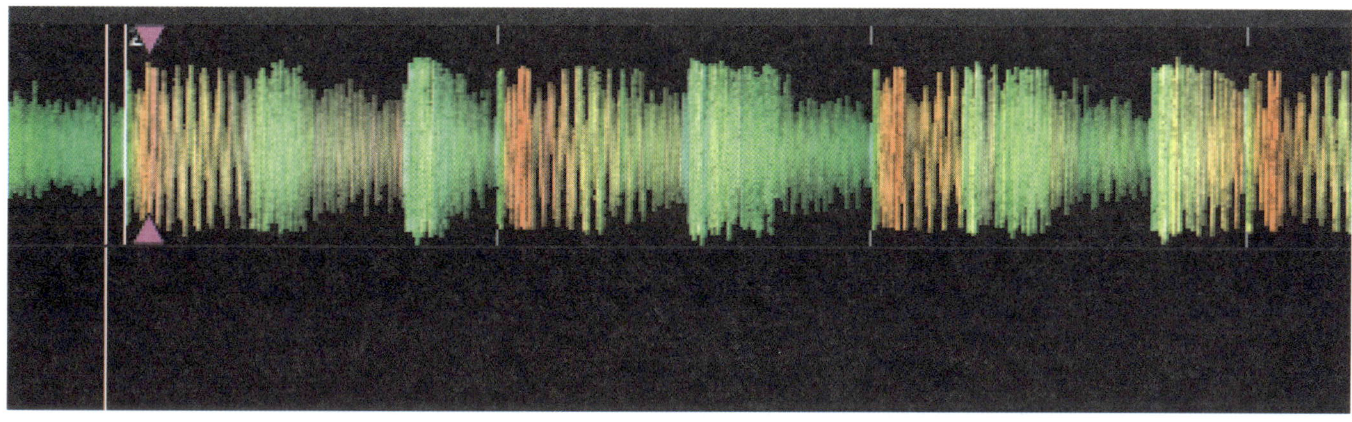

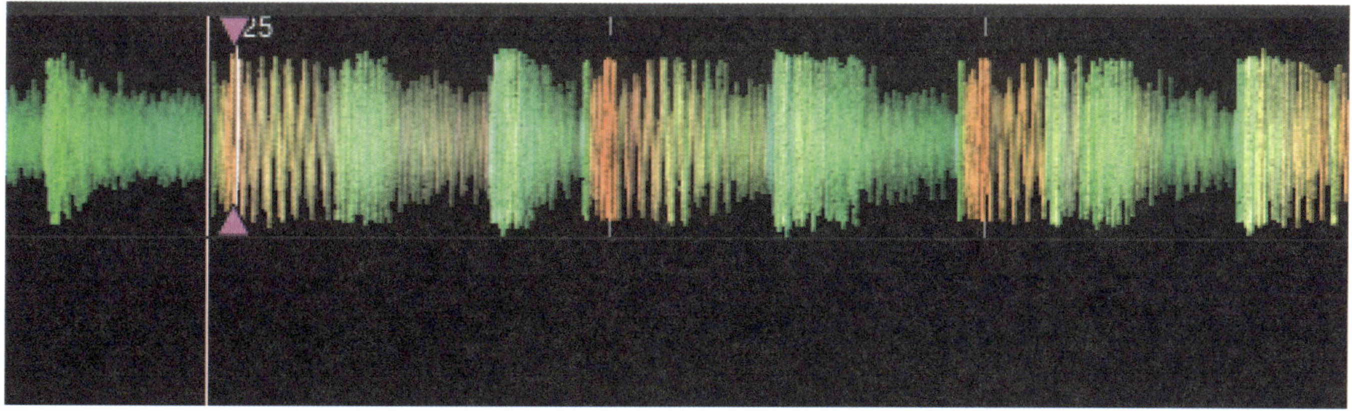

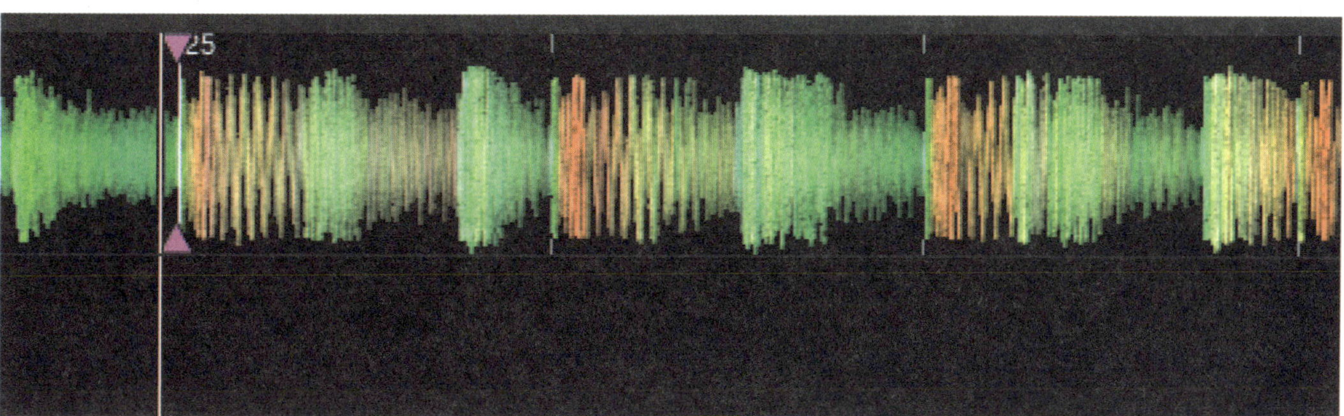